Intricate Patterns and Mandalas

Coloring Book for Adults
Lovink Coloring Books

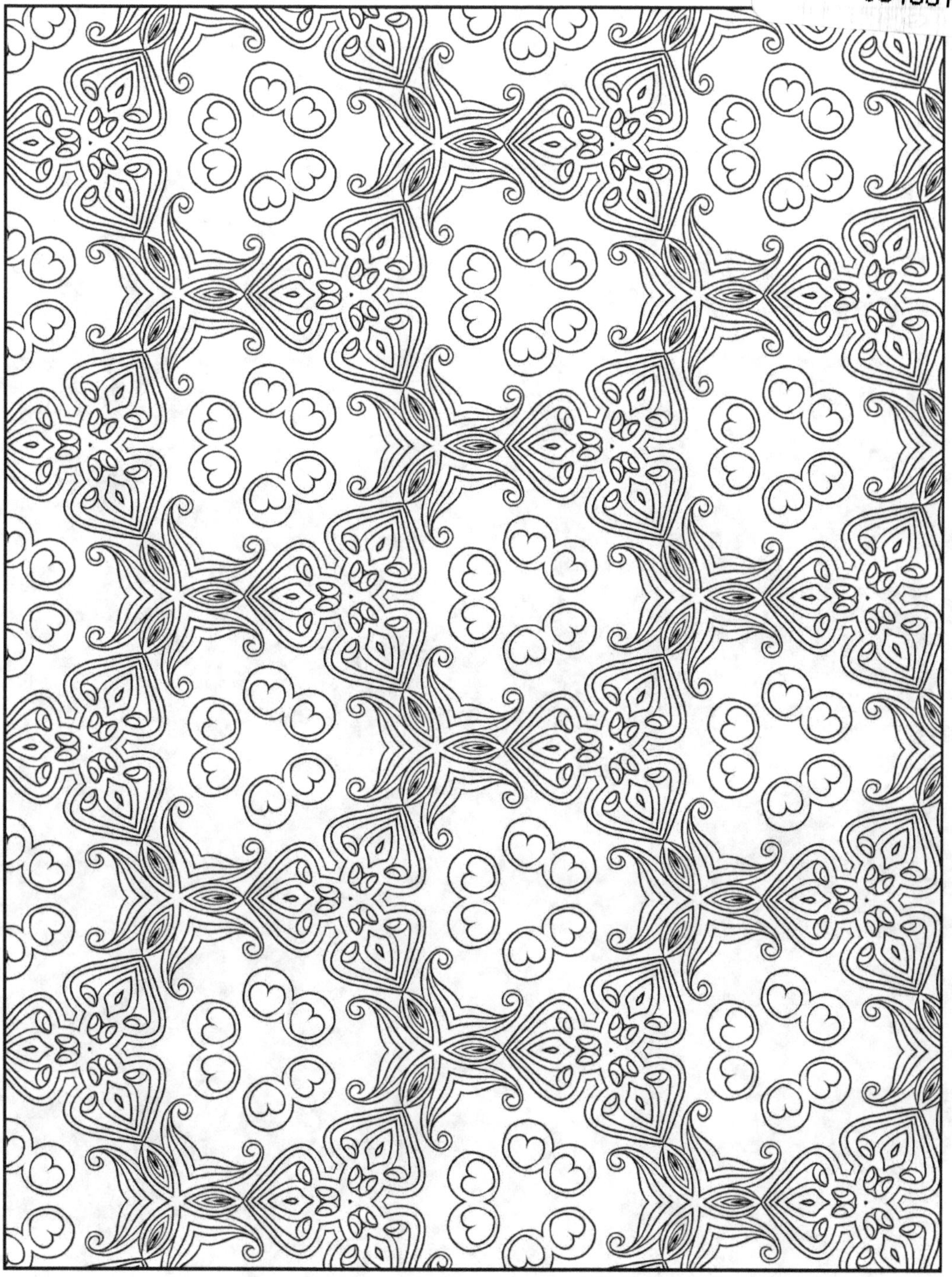

Olivia Johnson

Steps to a Relaxing Coloring

As an adult, you can enjoy coloring just as much as you did as a child. To make it a *truly relaxing experience*, try following these steps:

1. Find a quiet space. It's easier to focus on what you are doing when there are no distraction.

2. Organize your materials. Lay out your coloring book and crayons or pens.

3. Set the mood. Turn on some tranquil music, diffuse lavender or another relaxing oil and make sure you have your preferred drink at hand.

4. Select your picture. Which image speaks to you today? That's the one you should color.

5. Choose your palette. Select the colors you will be using for your image.

6. Begin coloring. This is the fun part. Don't worry about getting everything perfect, just start.

Allow yourself to relax and focus on the coloring. You'll find it is an amazing way to alleviate stress and take a little time out from the day's hassles. If you feel don't want to do it anymore, just stop!

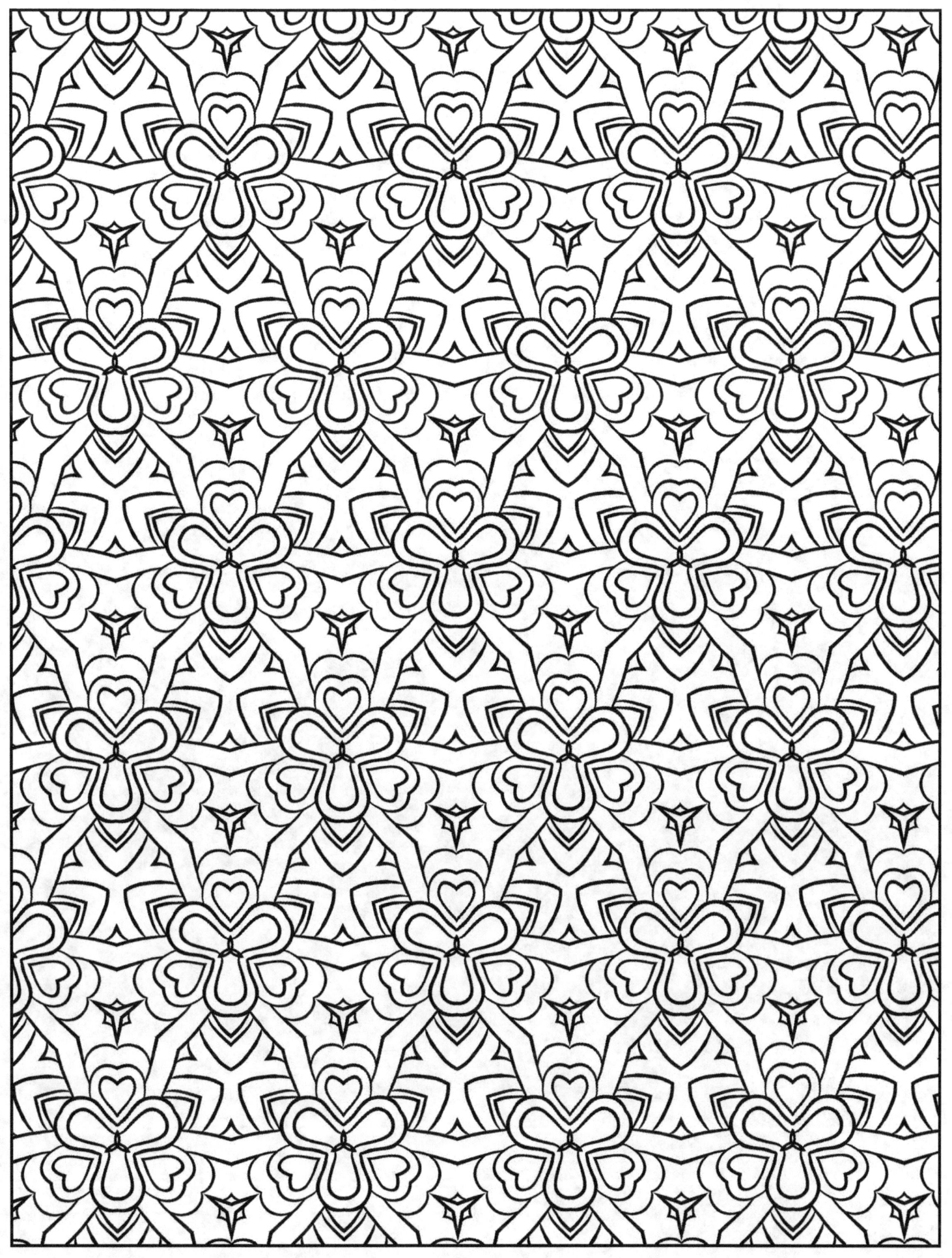

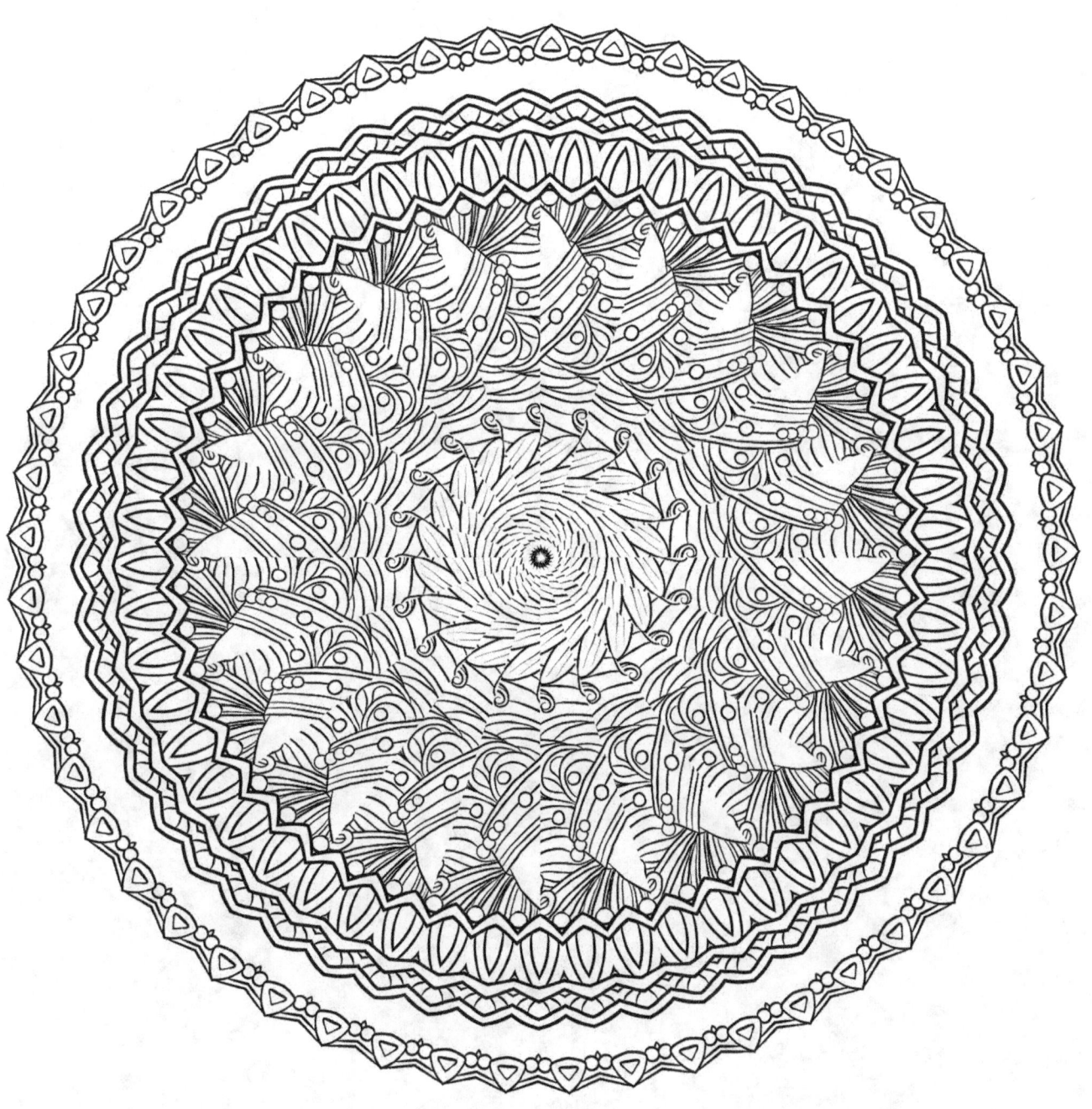

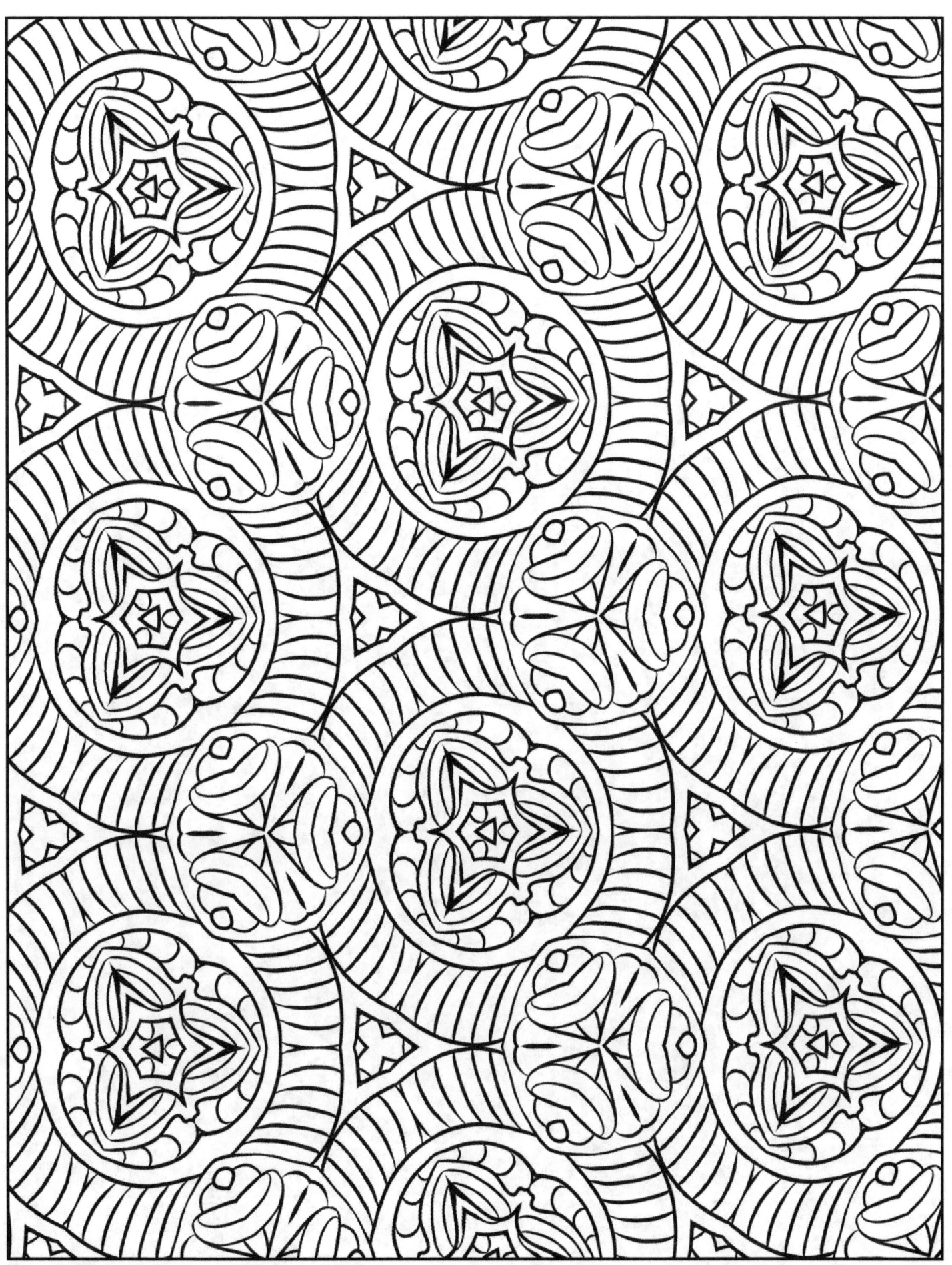

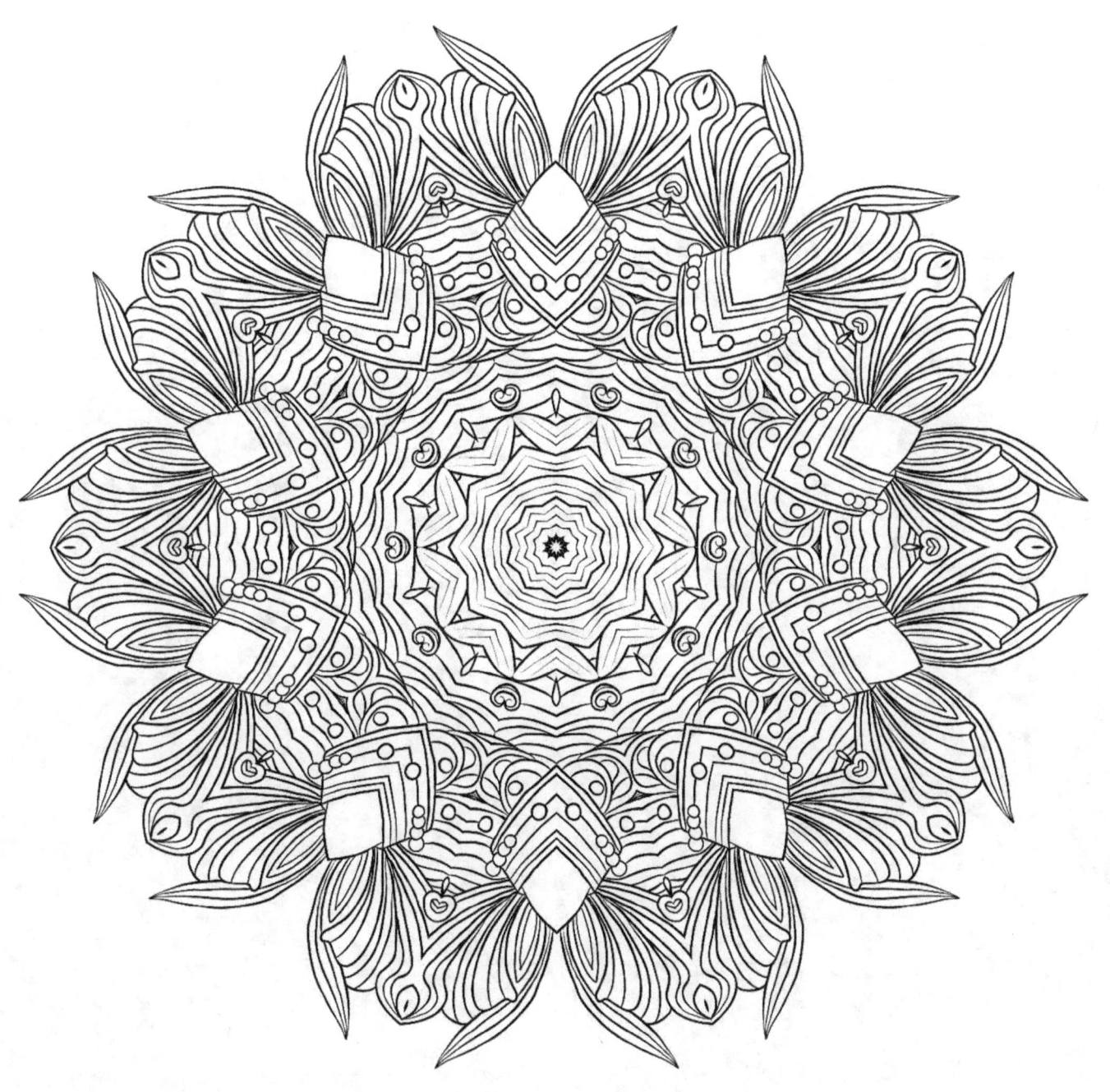

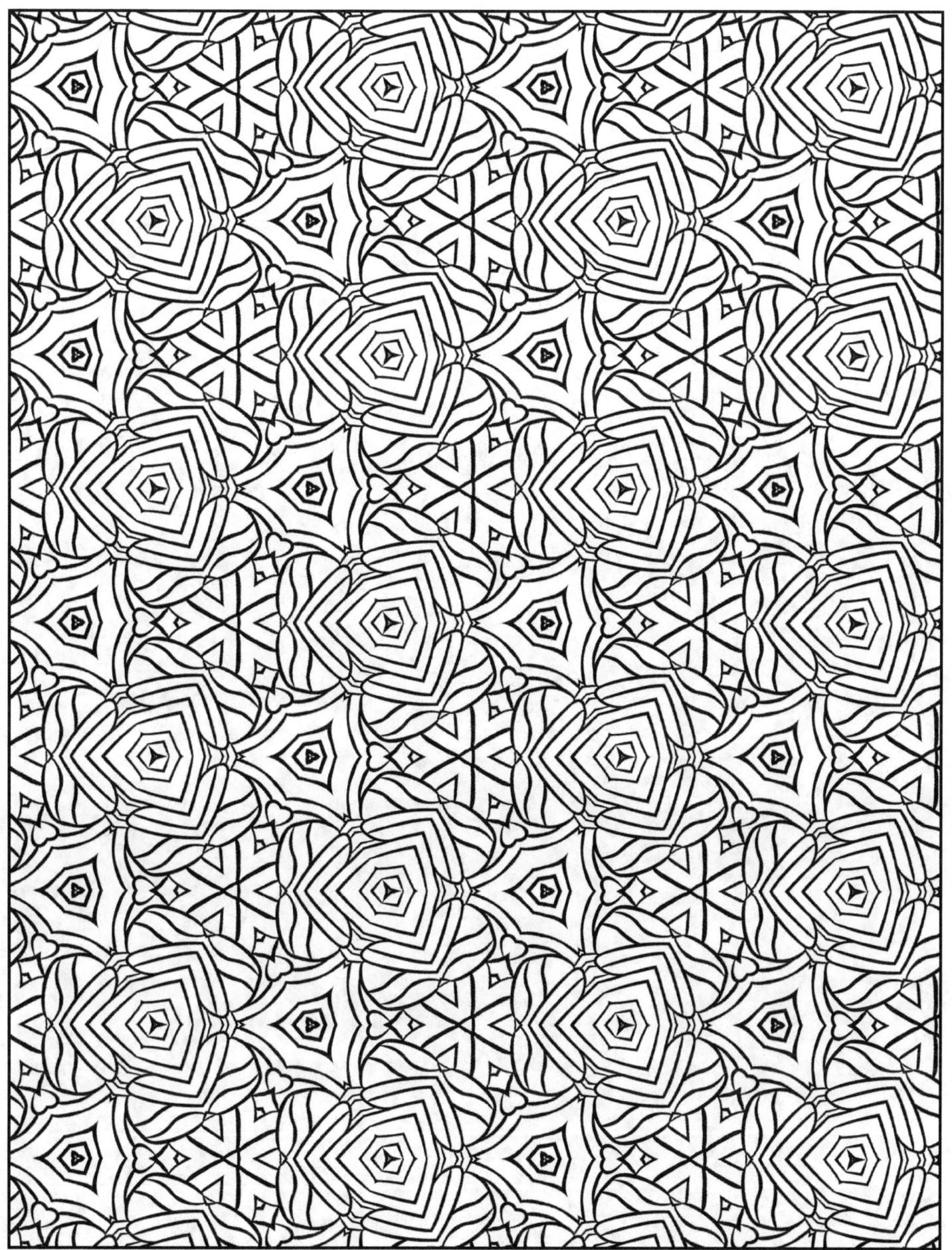

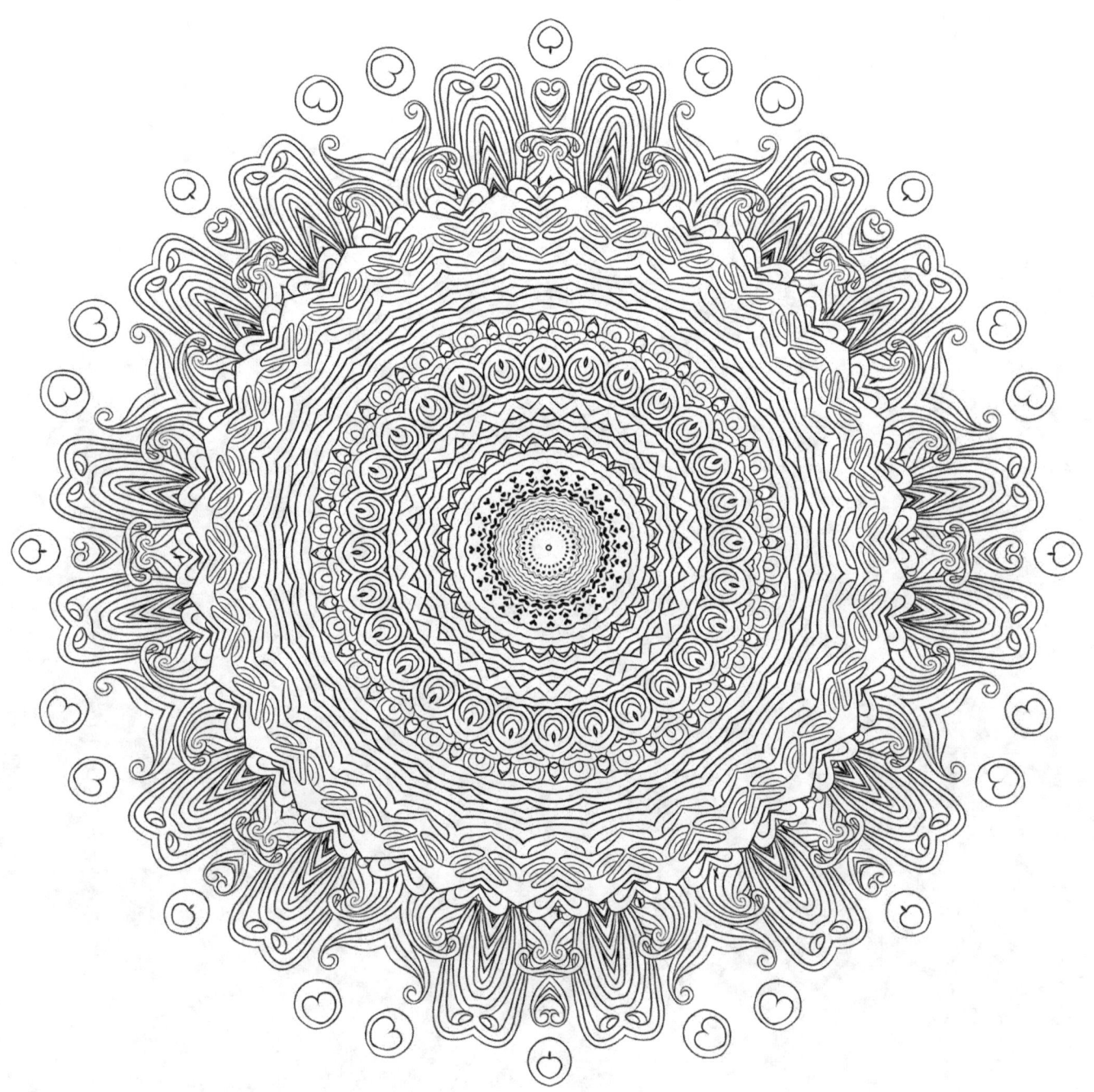

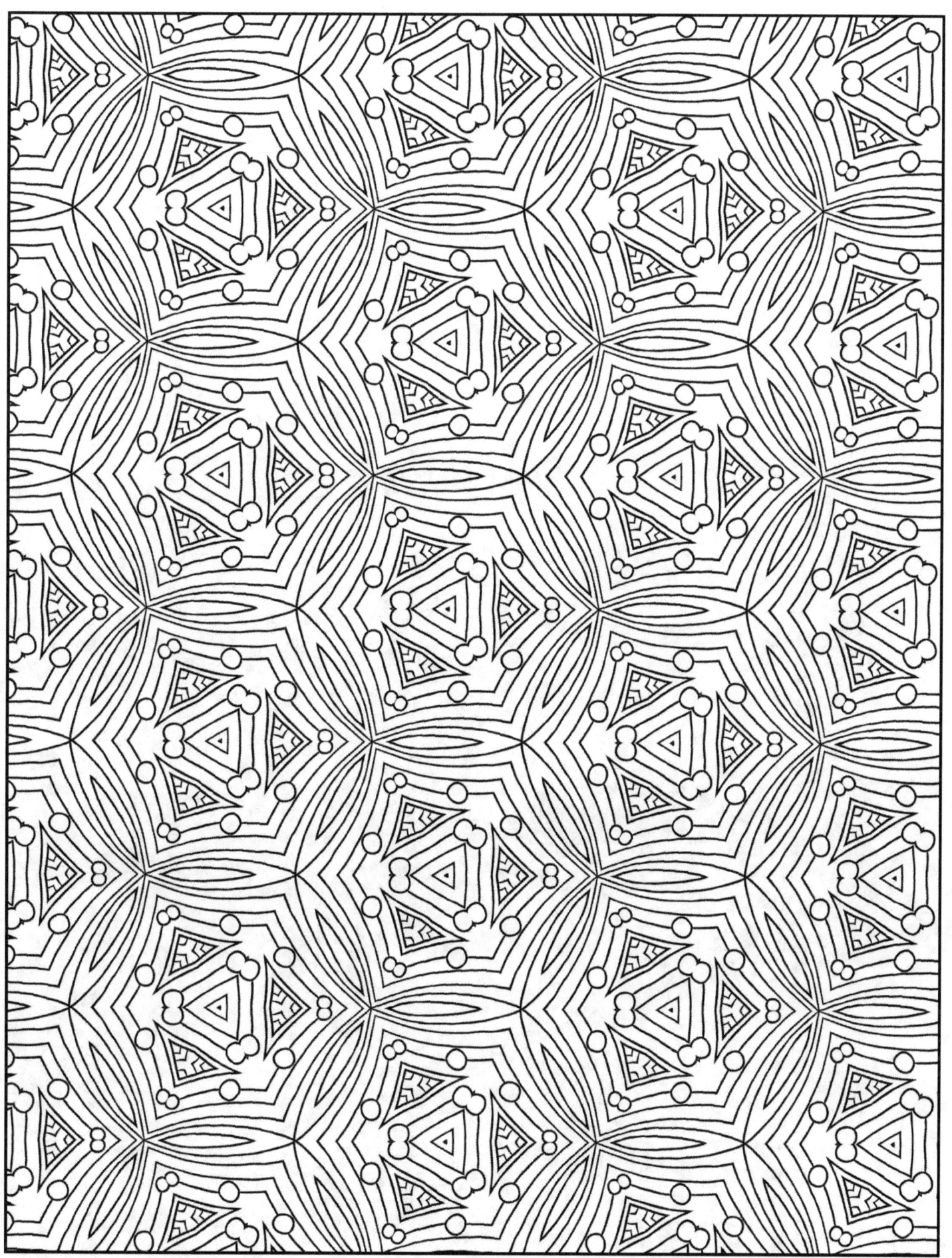

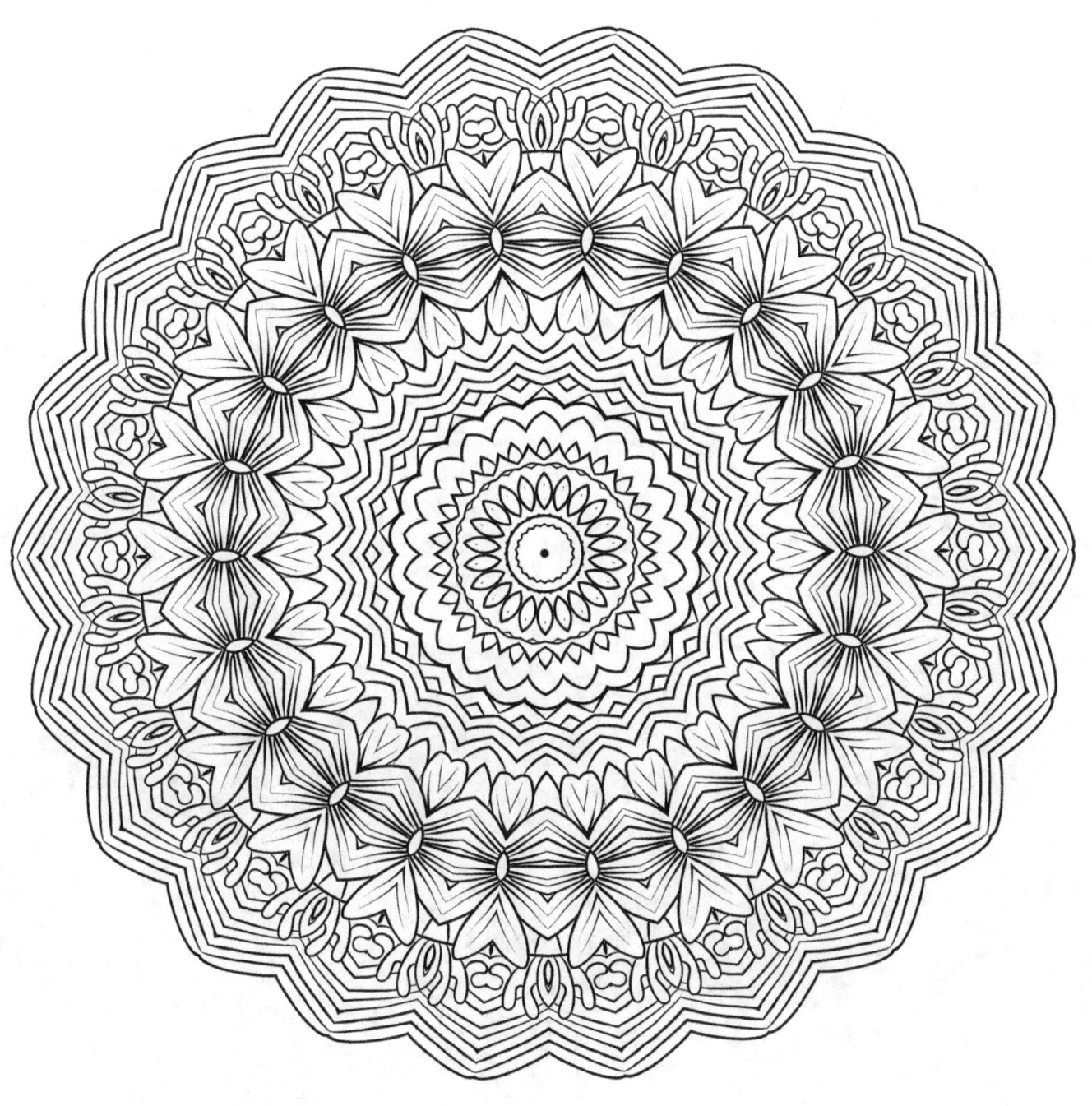

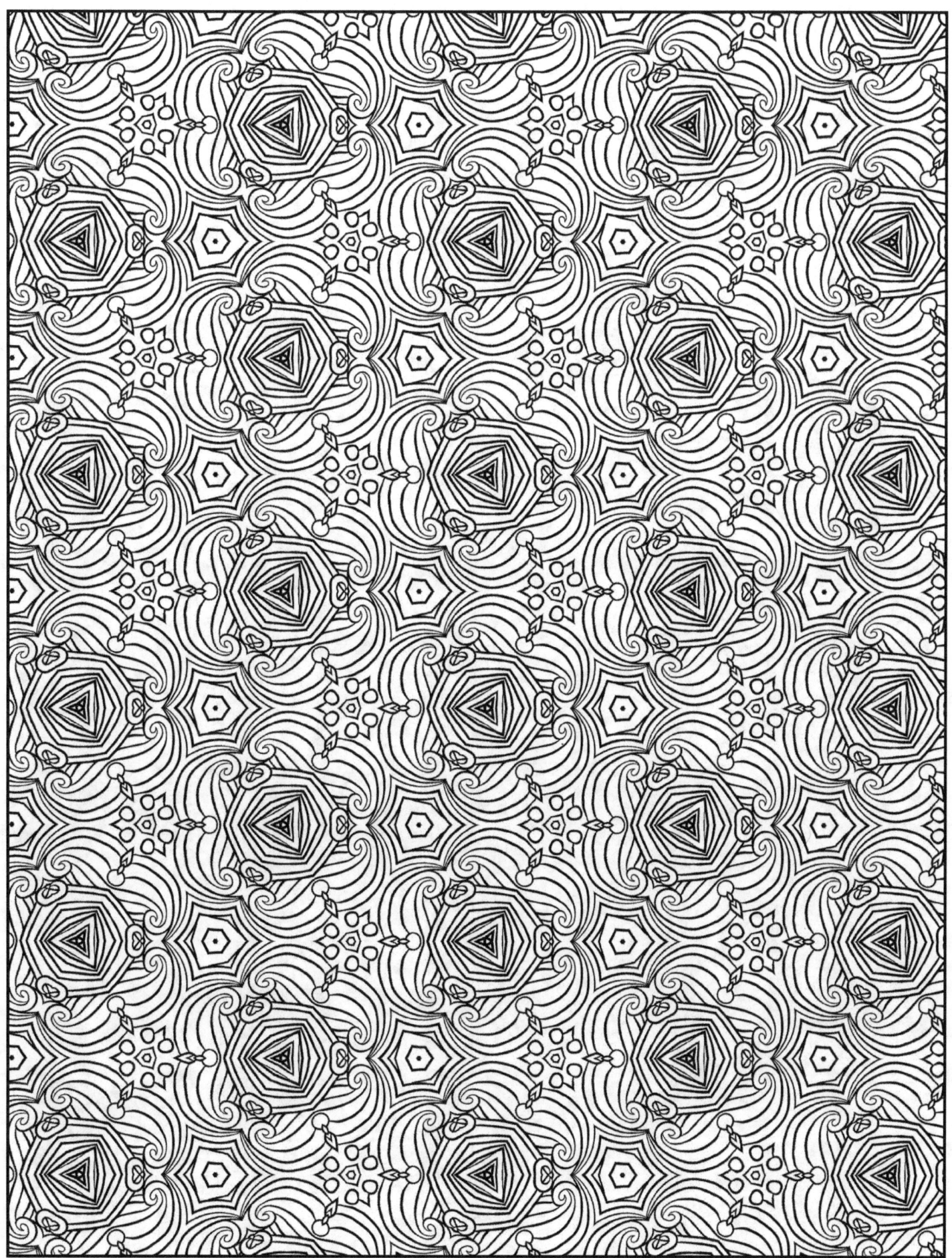

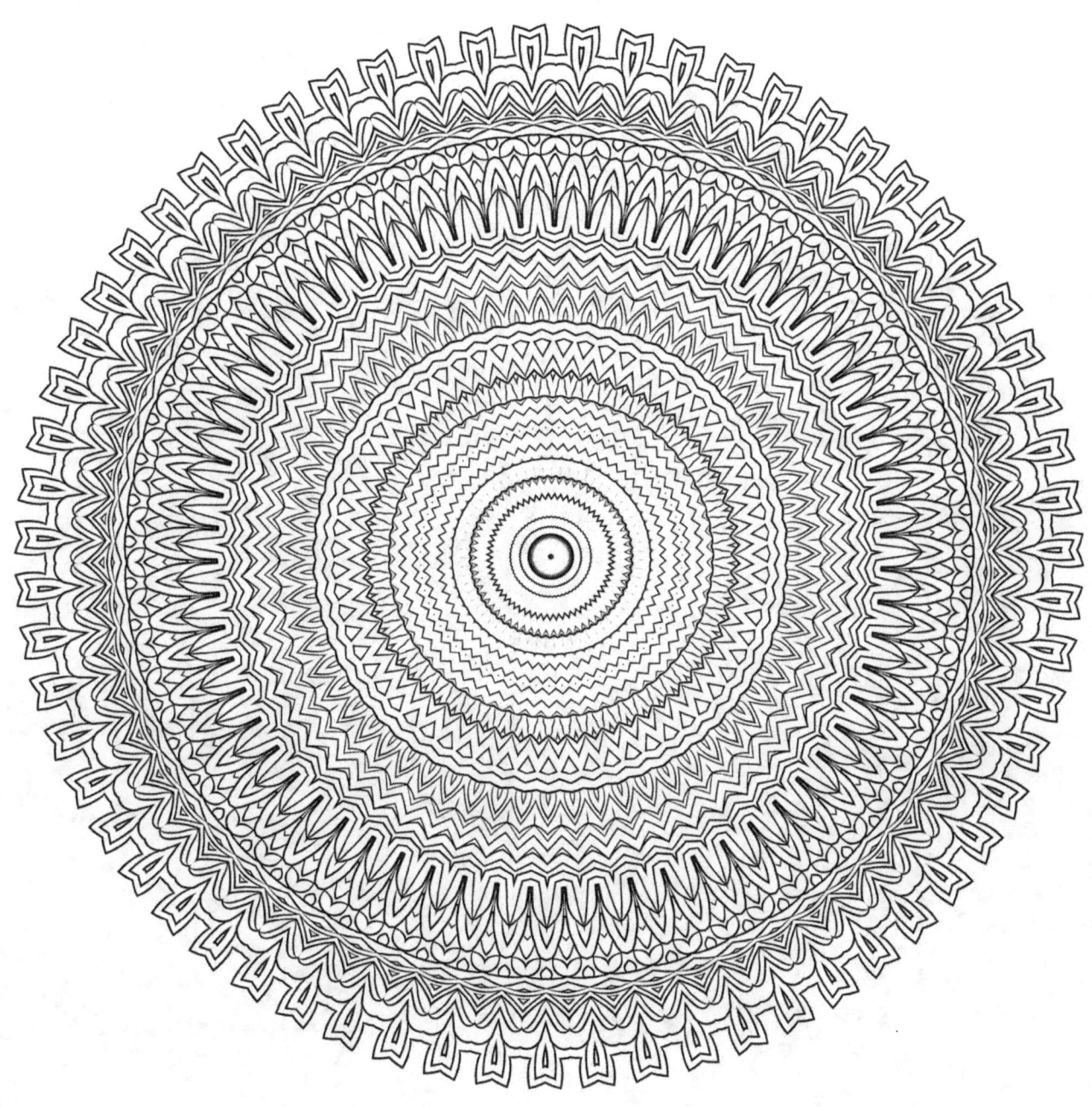

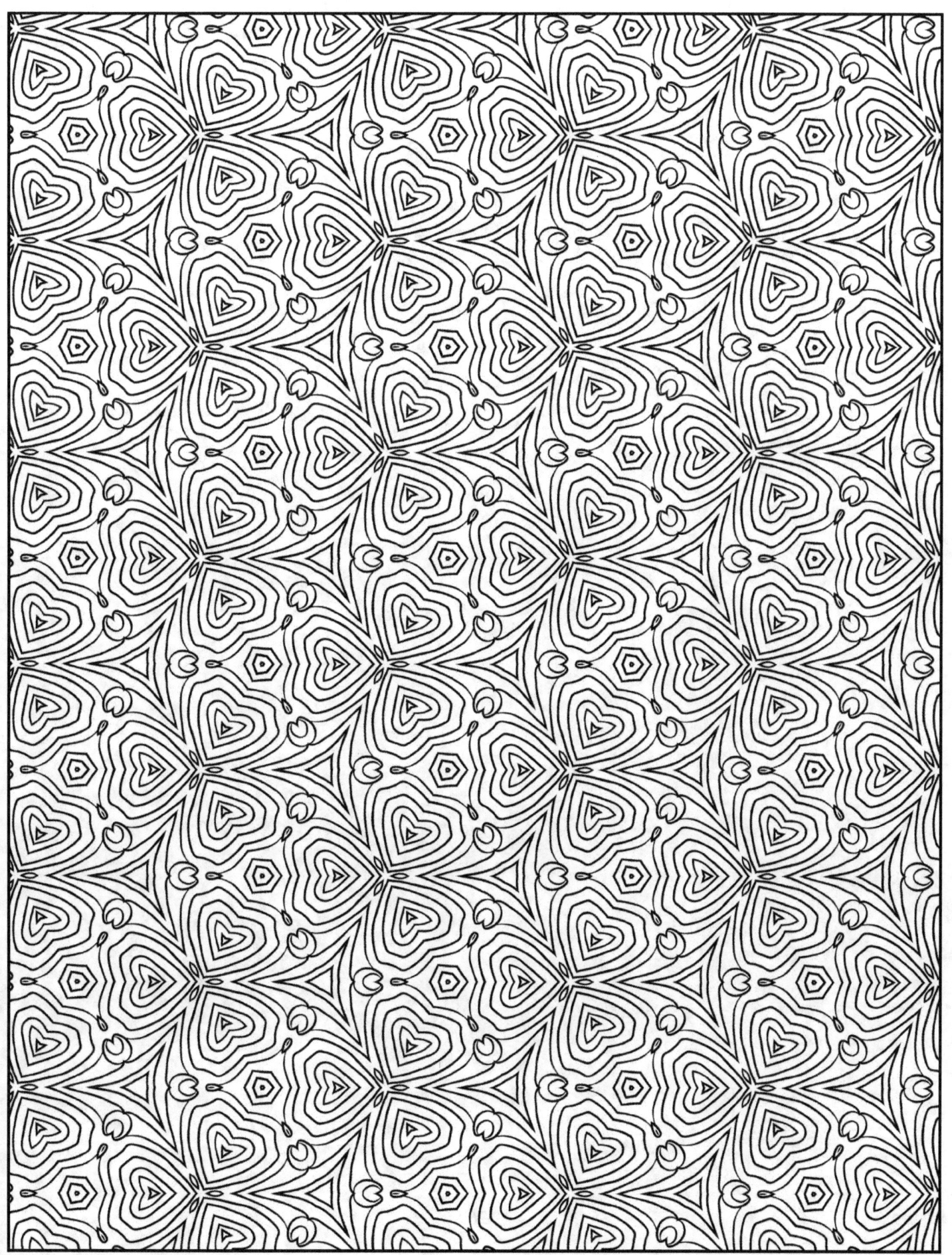

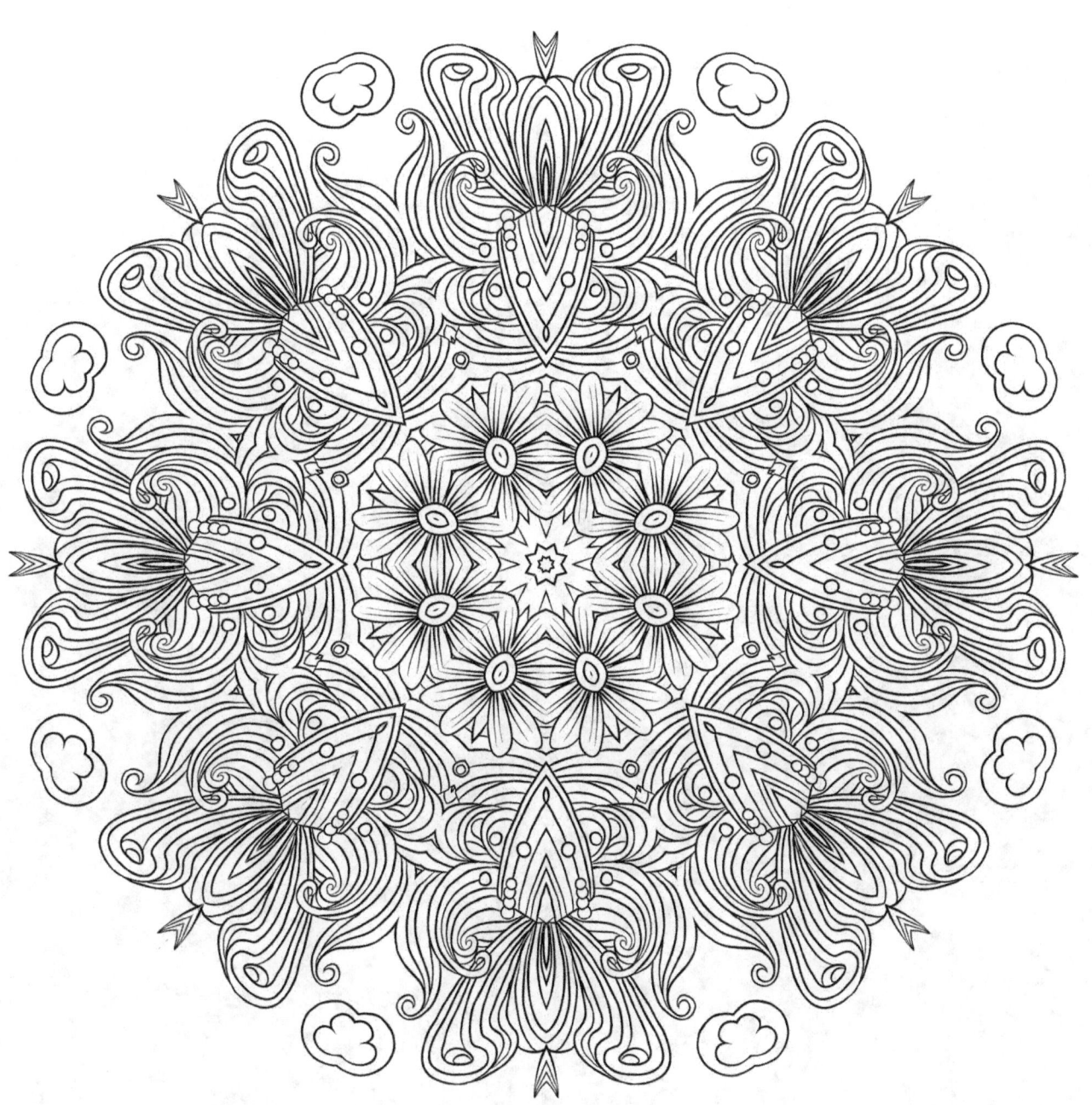

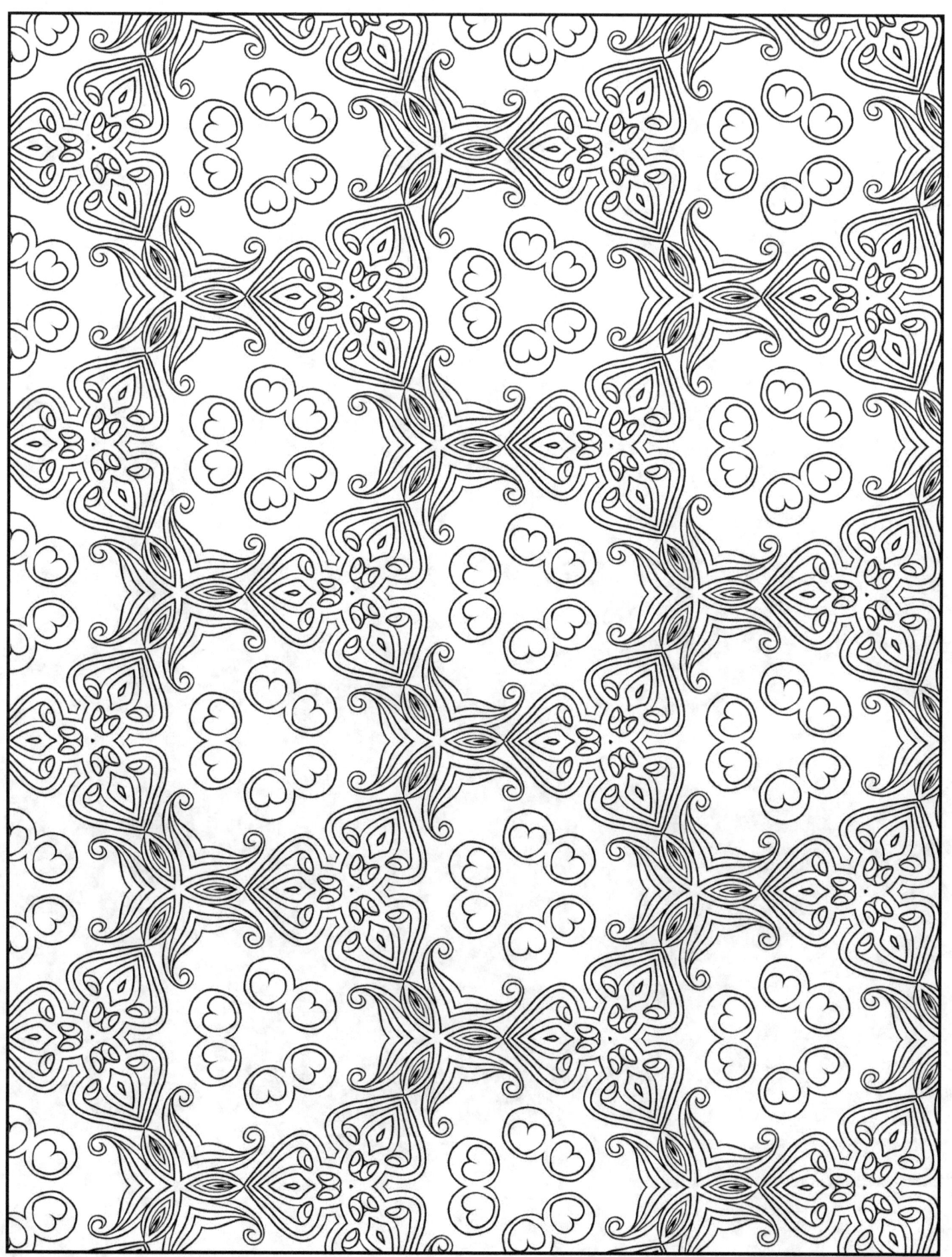

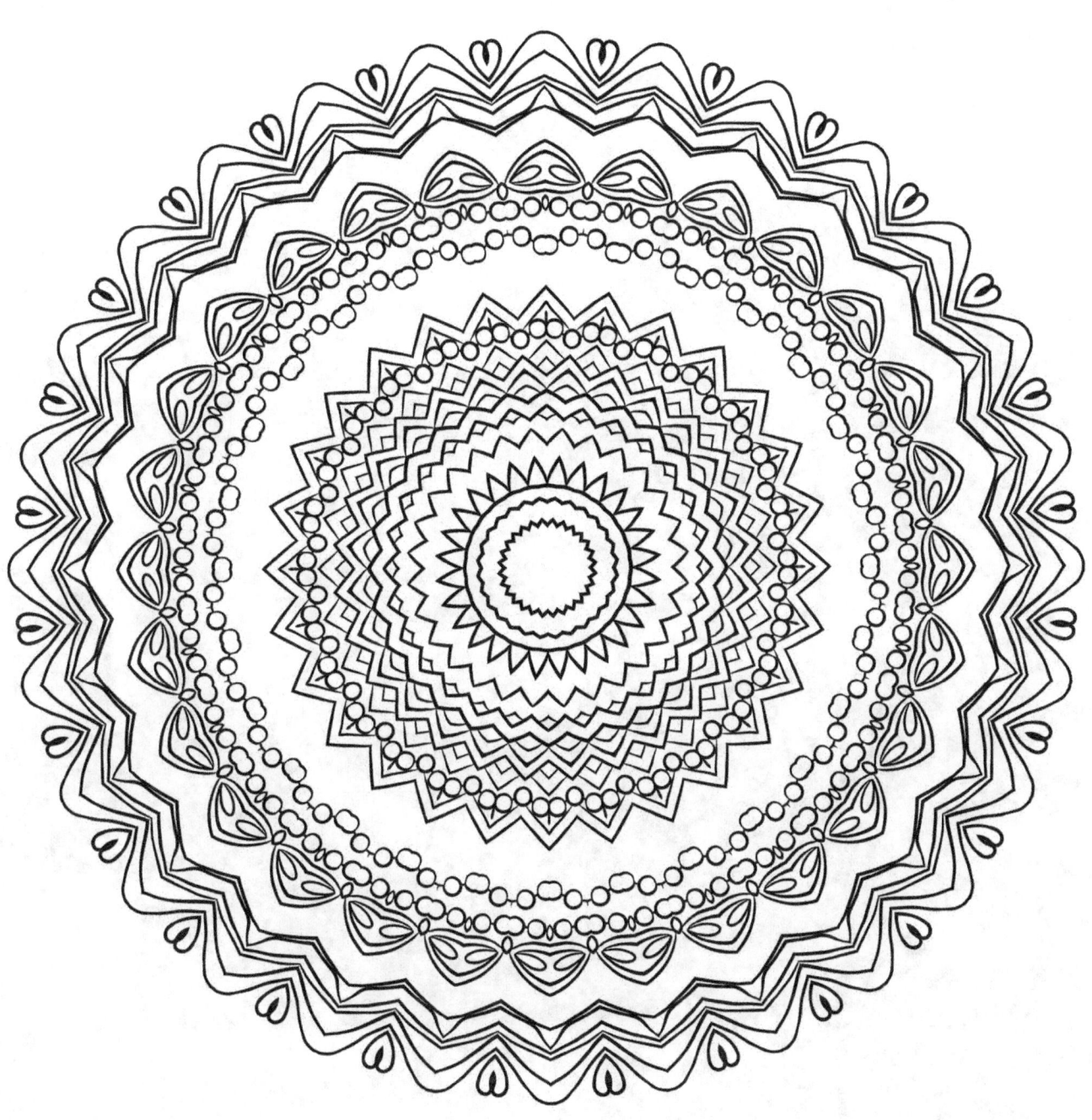

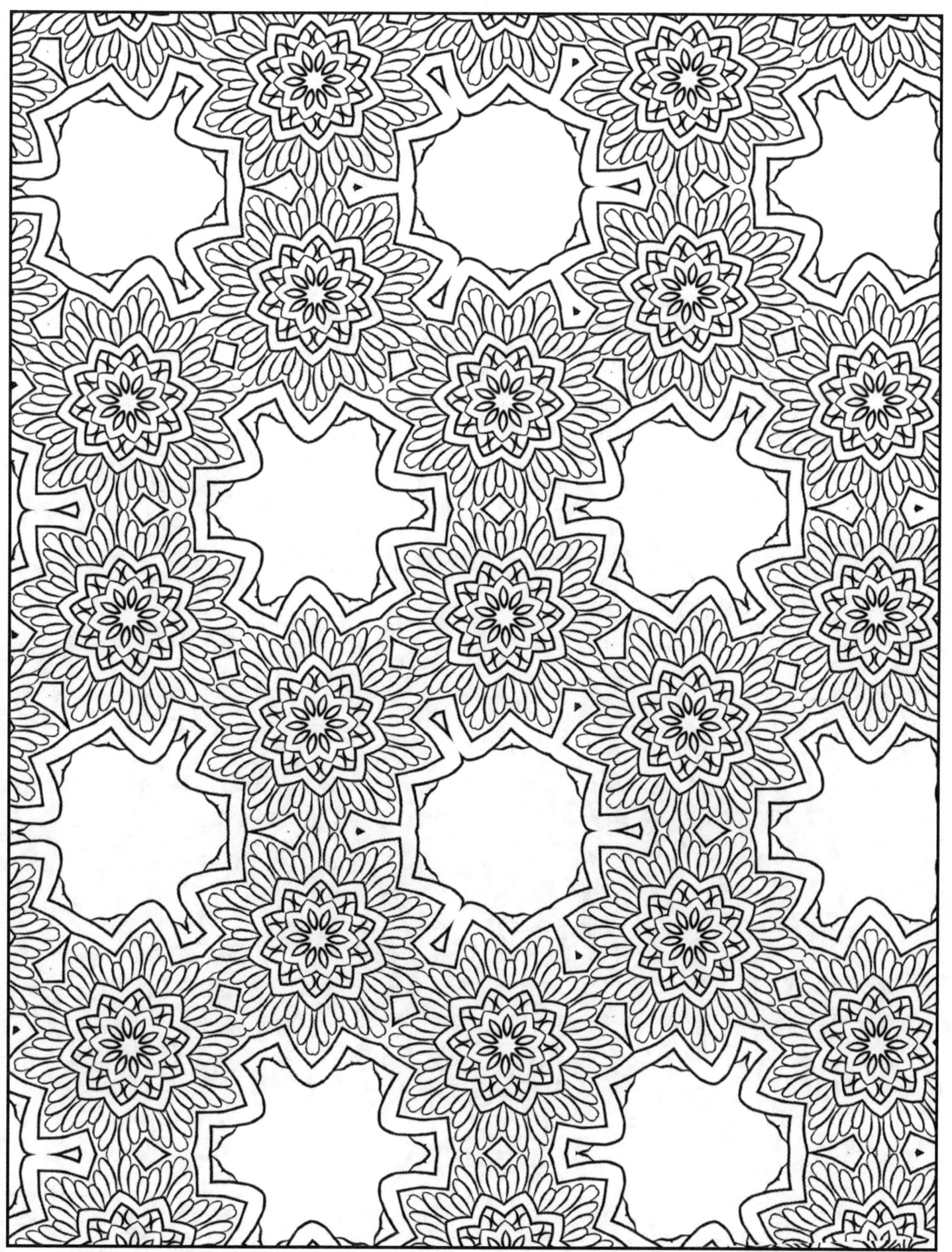

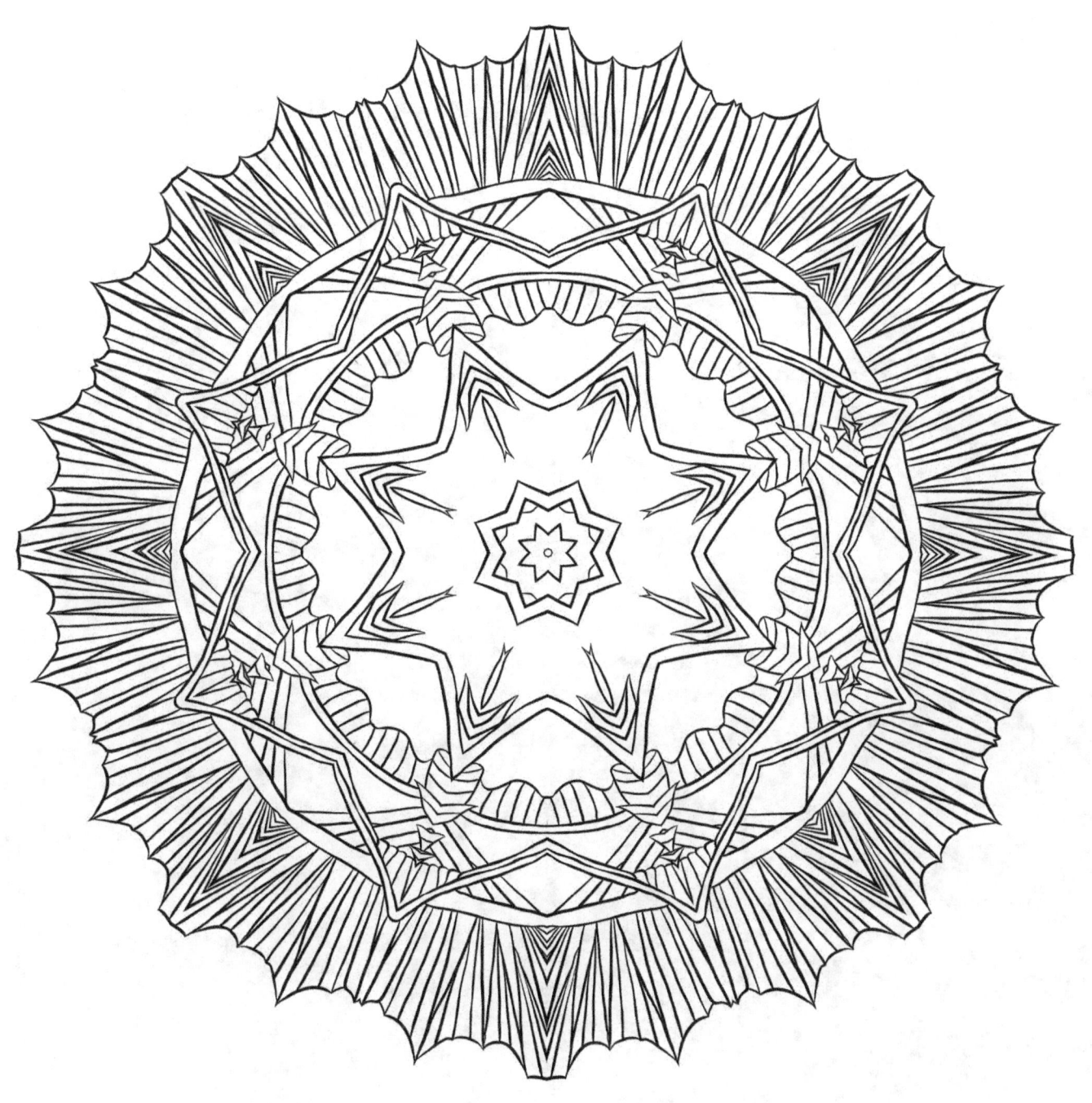

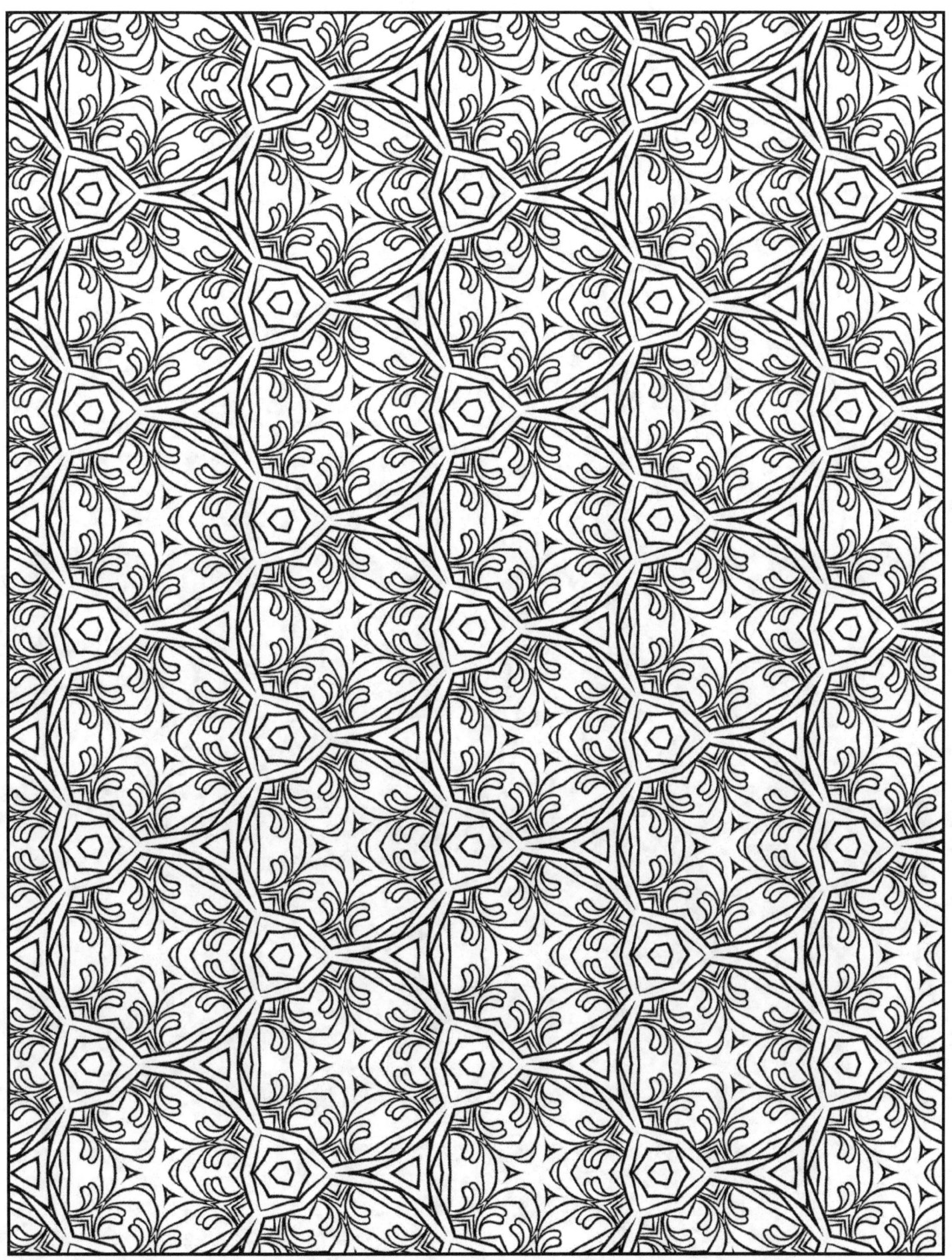

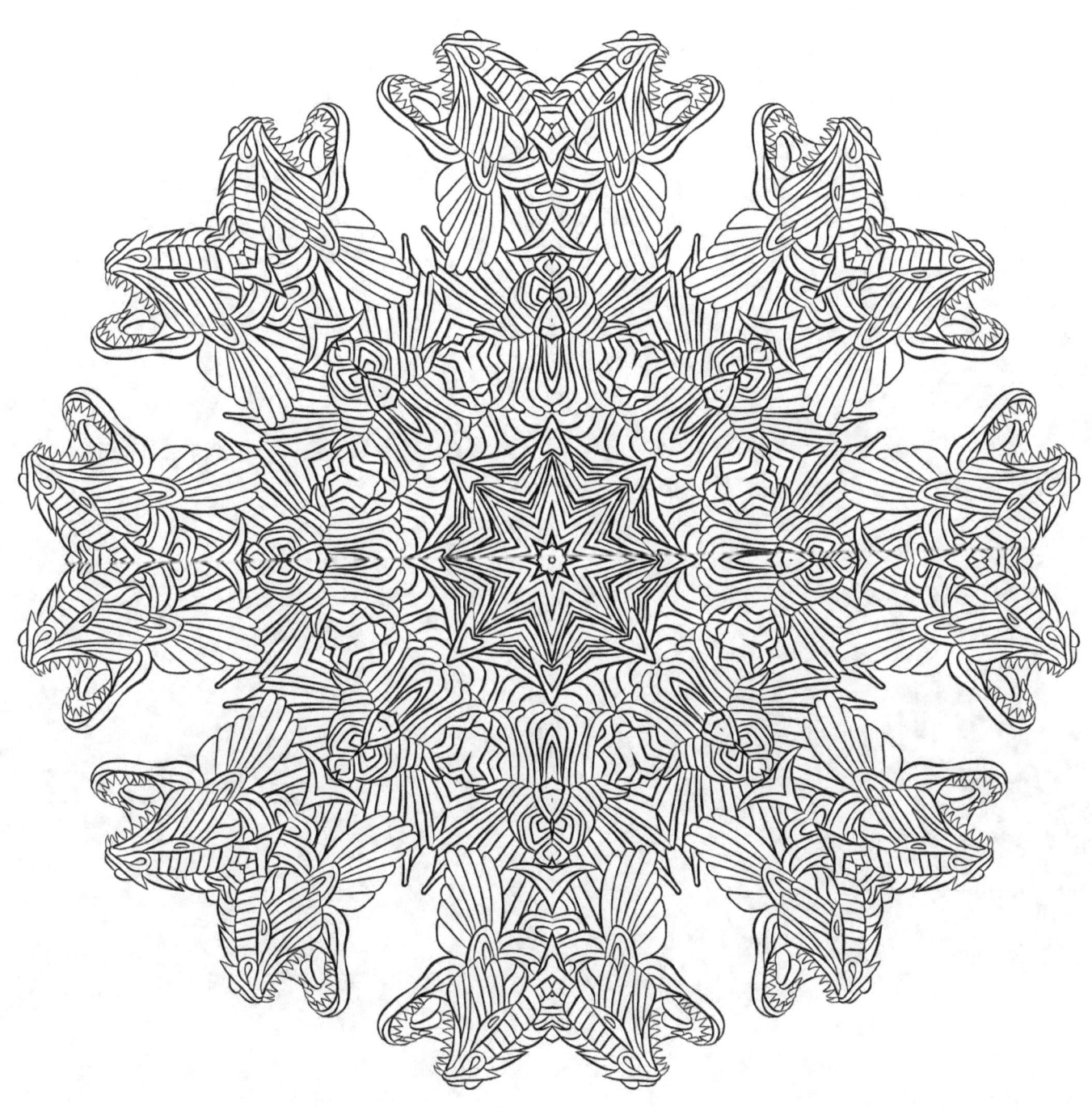

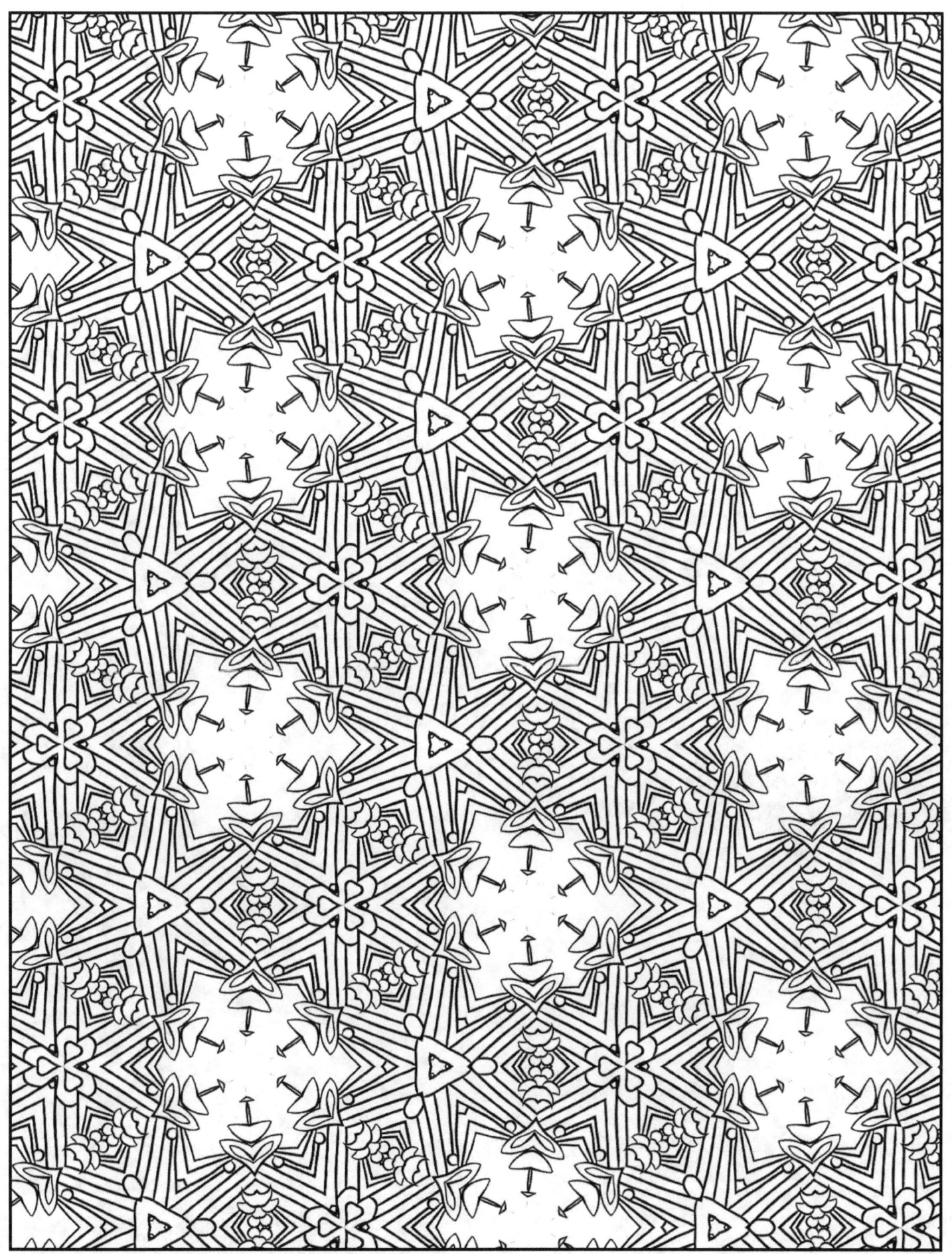

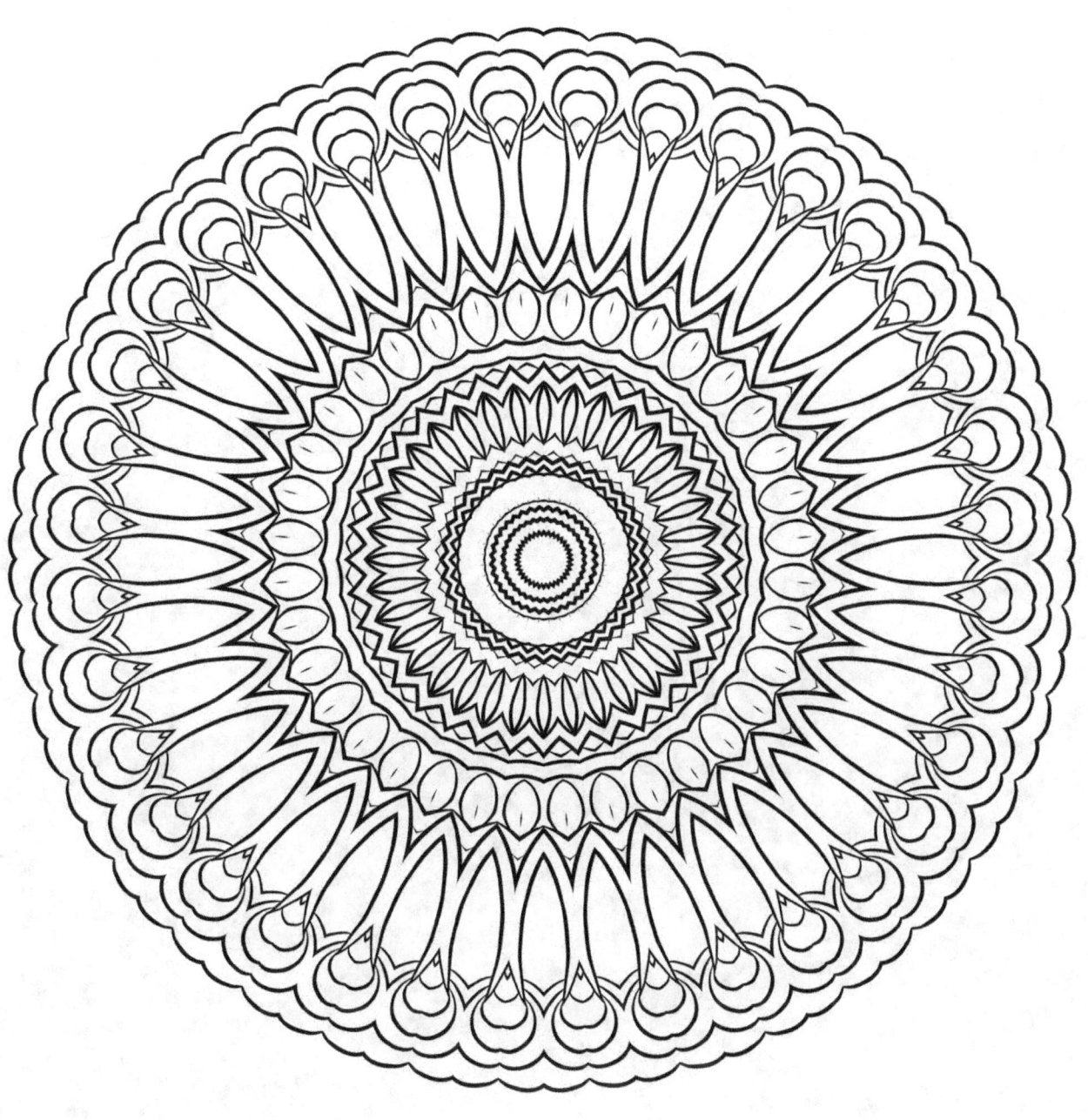

44

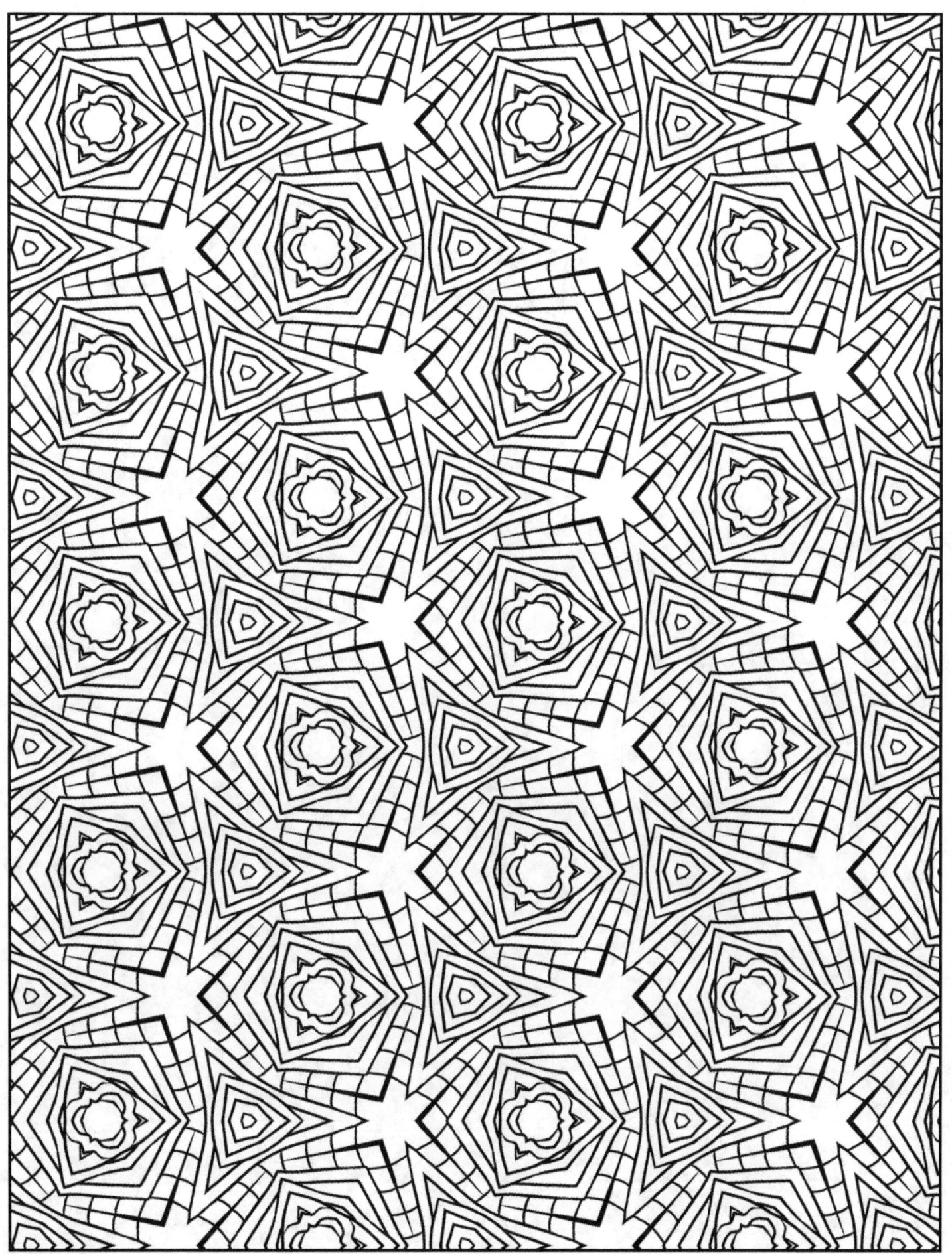

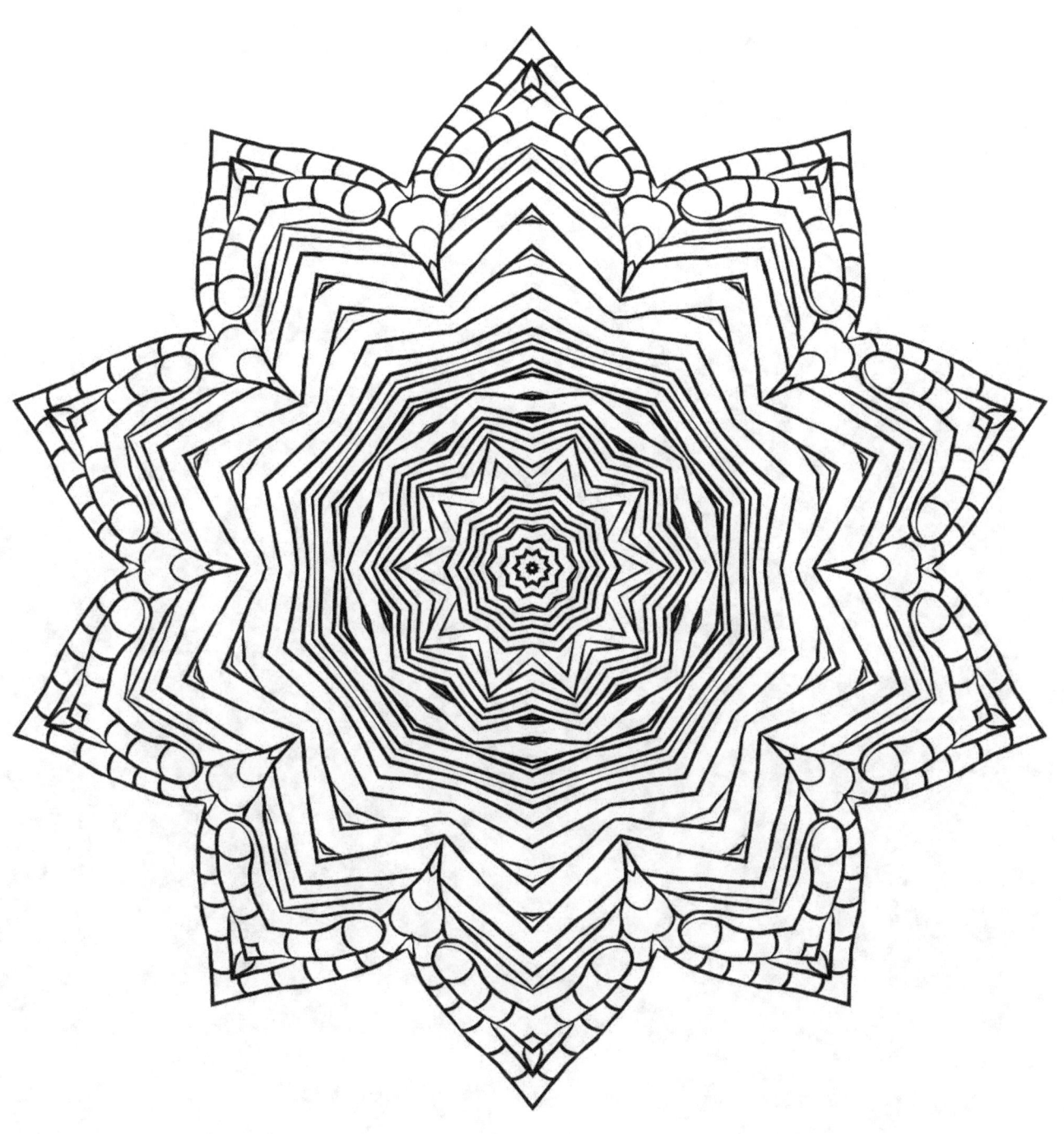

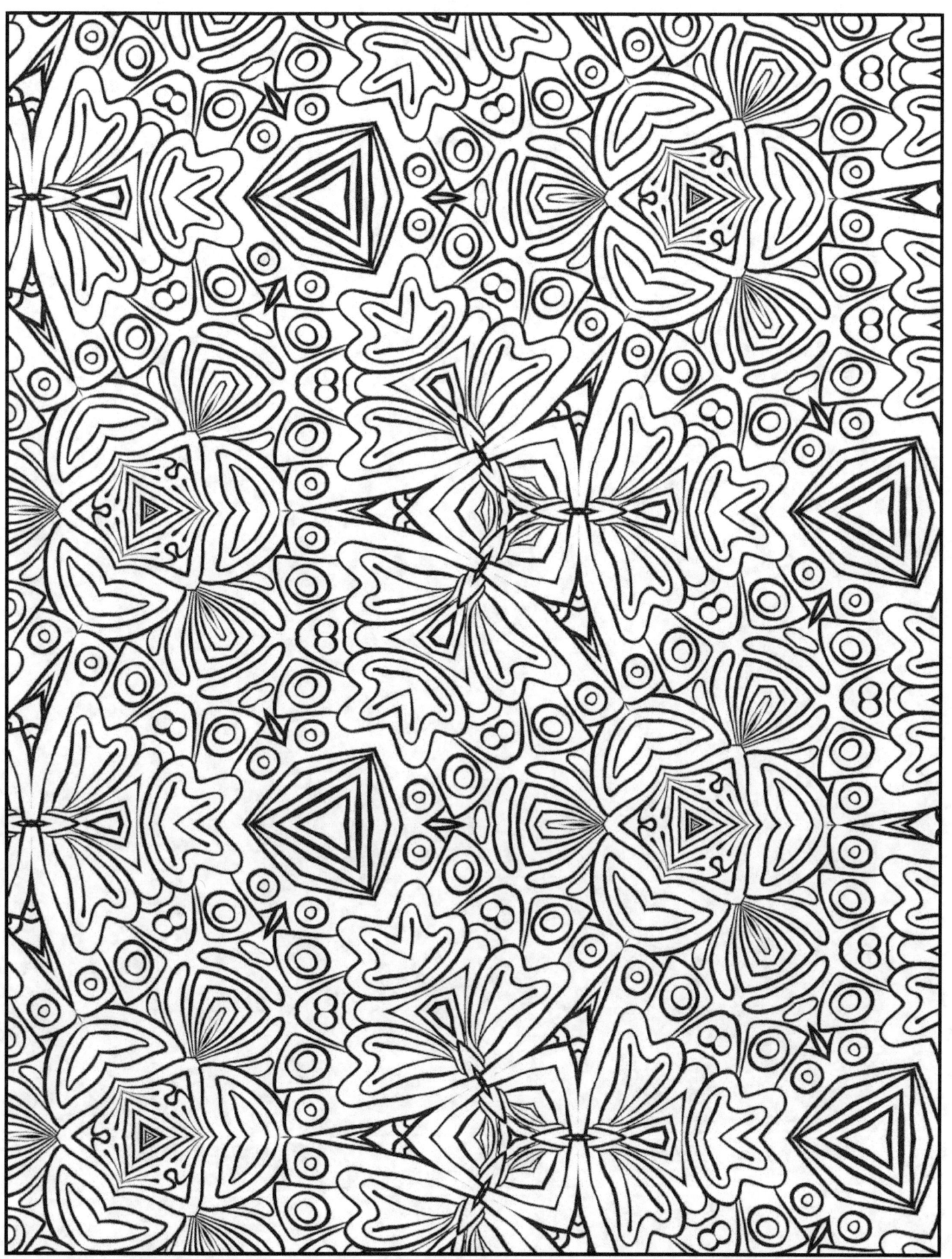

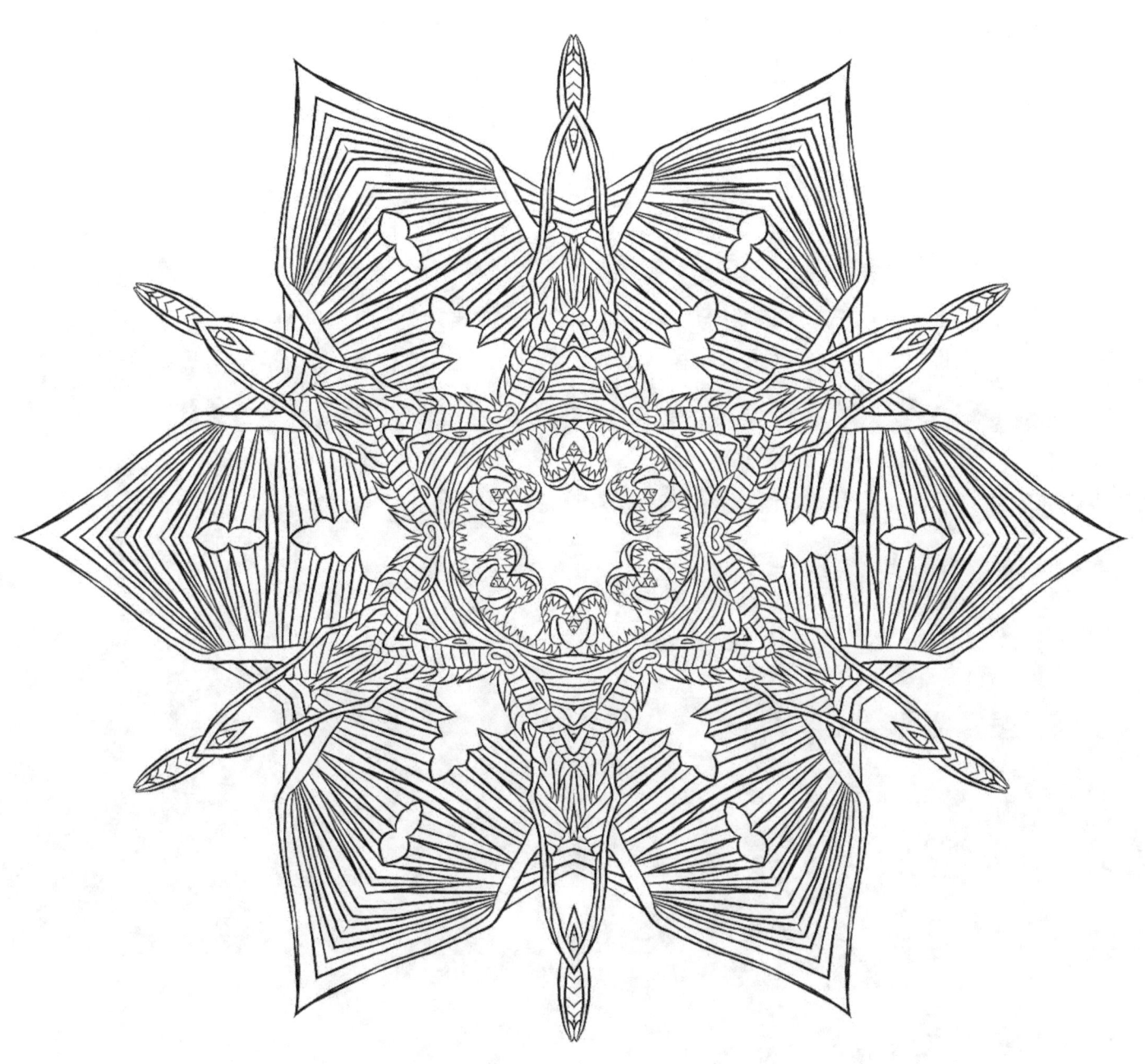

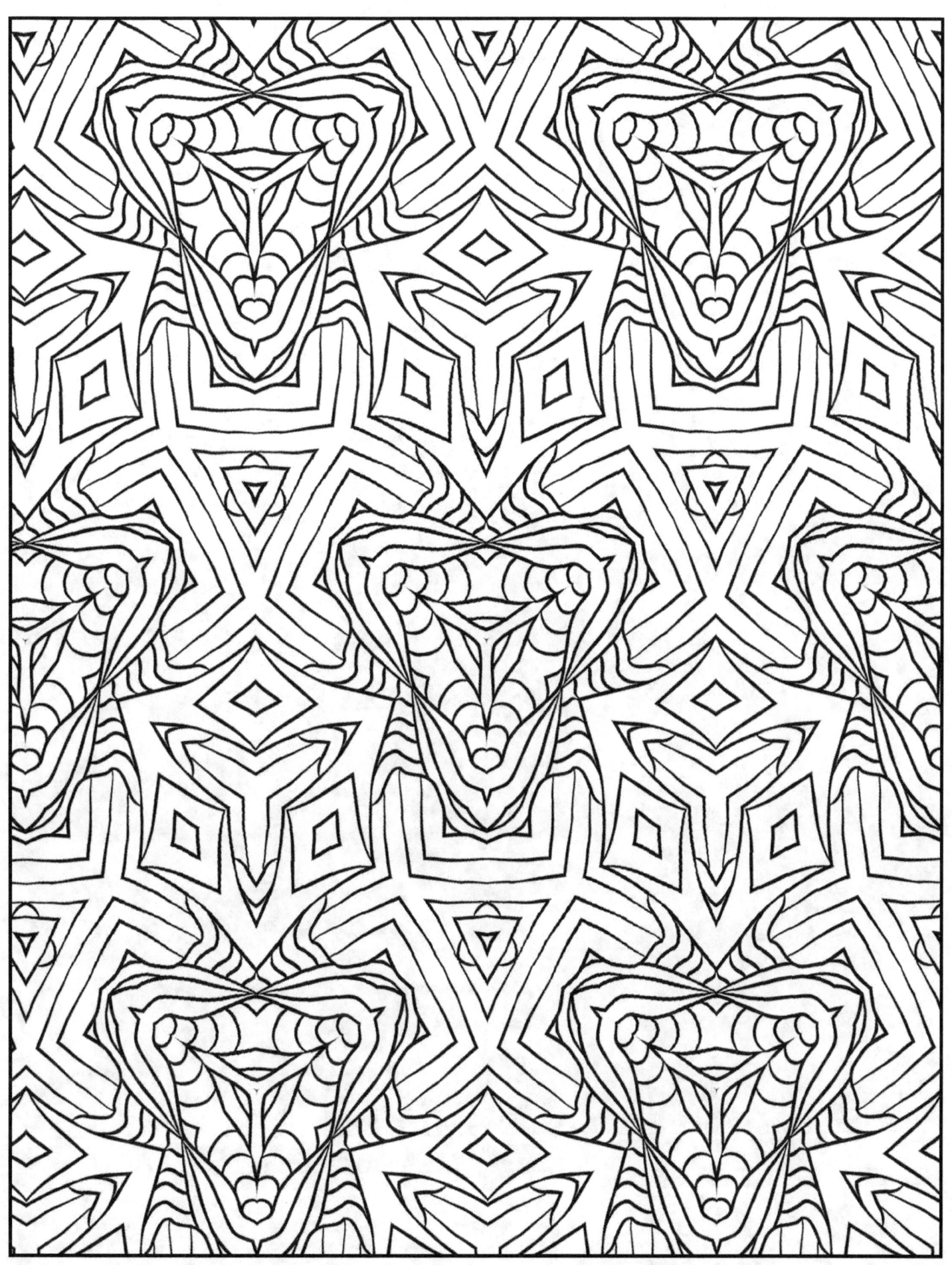

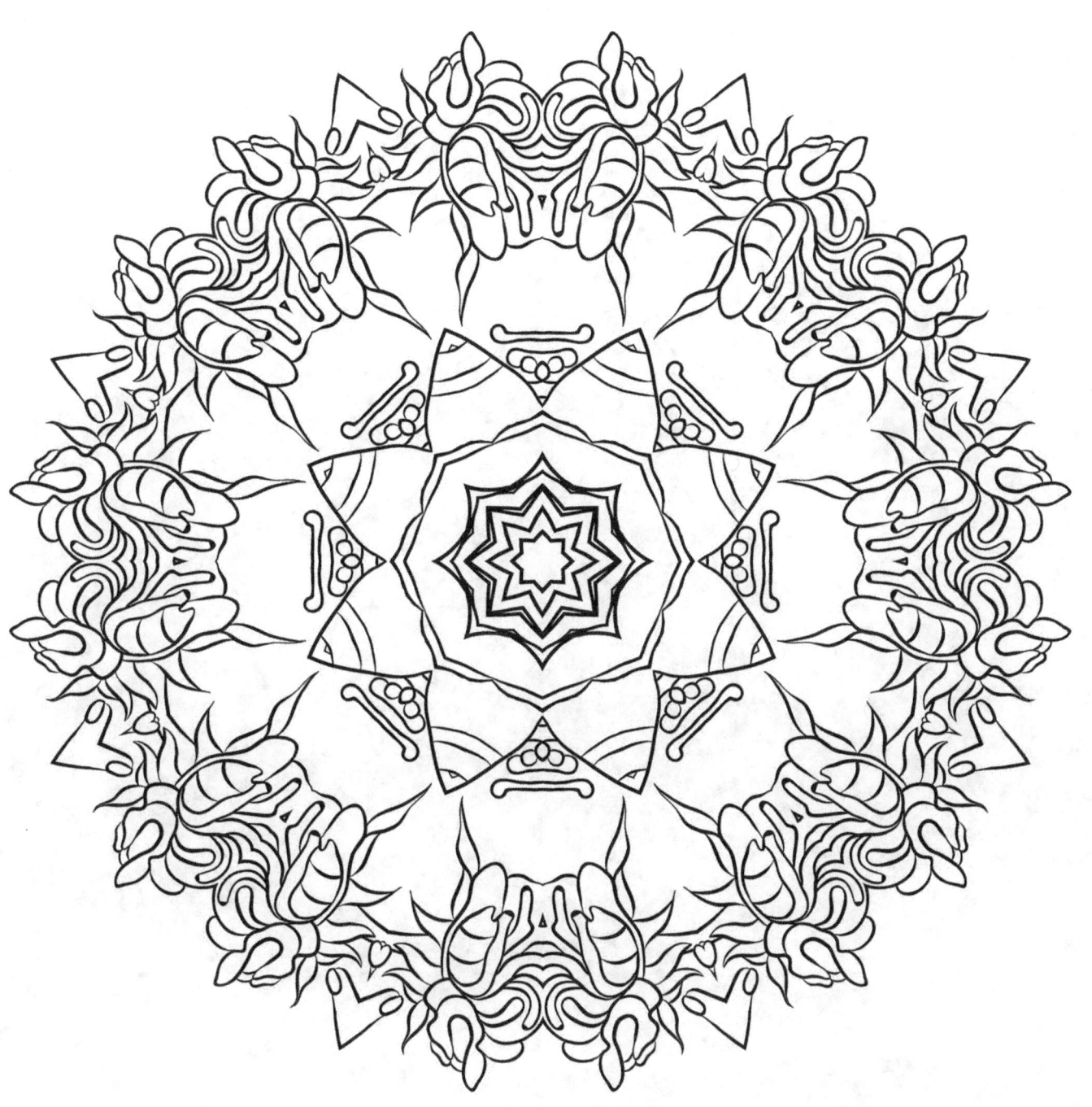

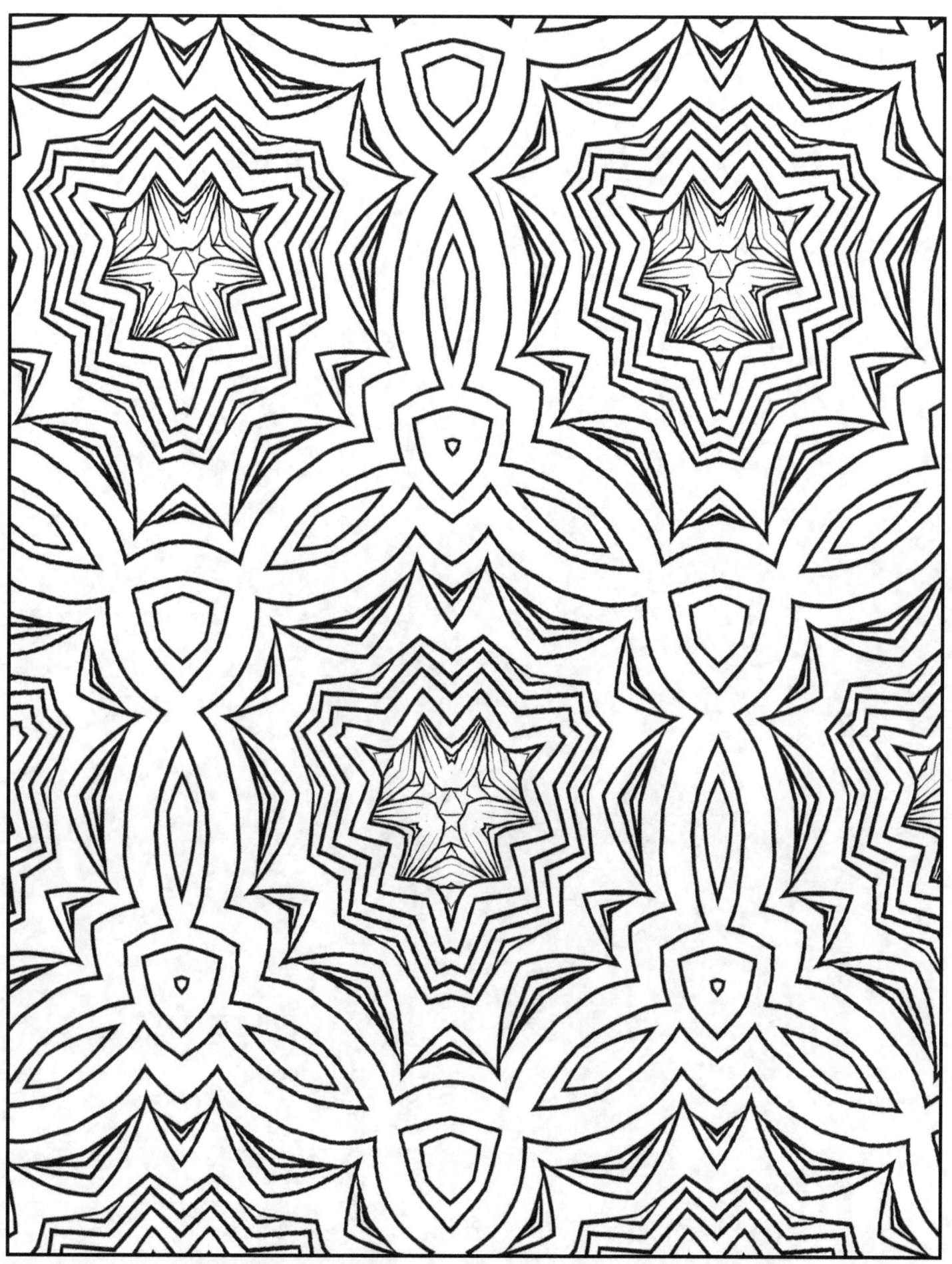

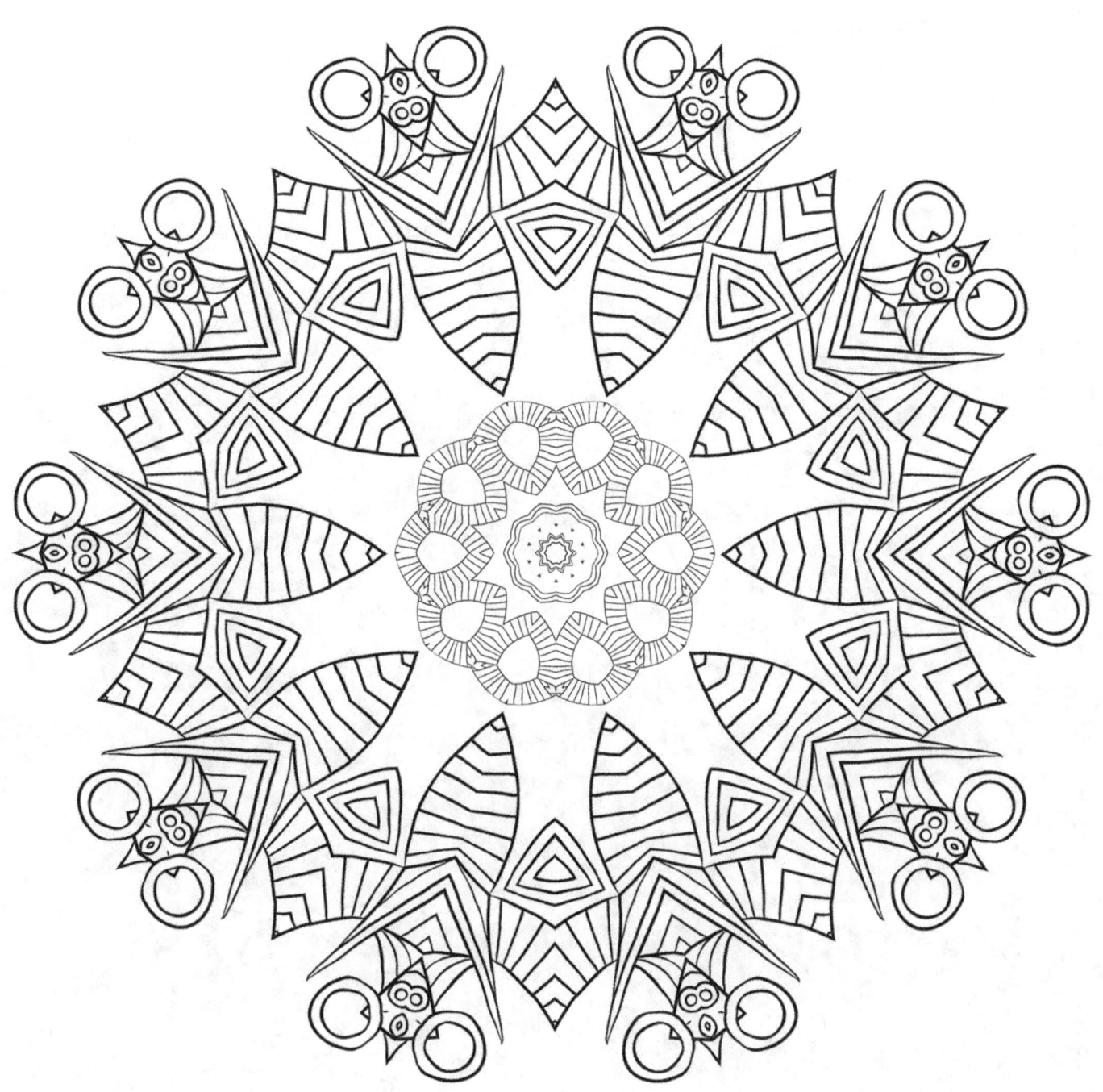

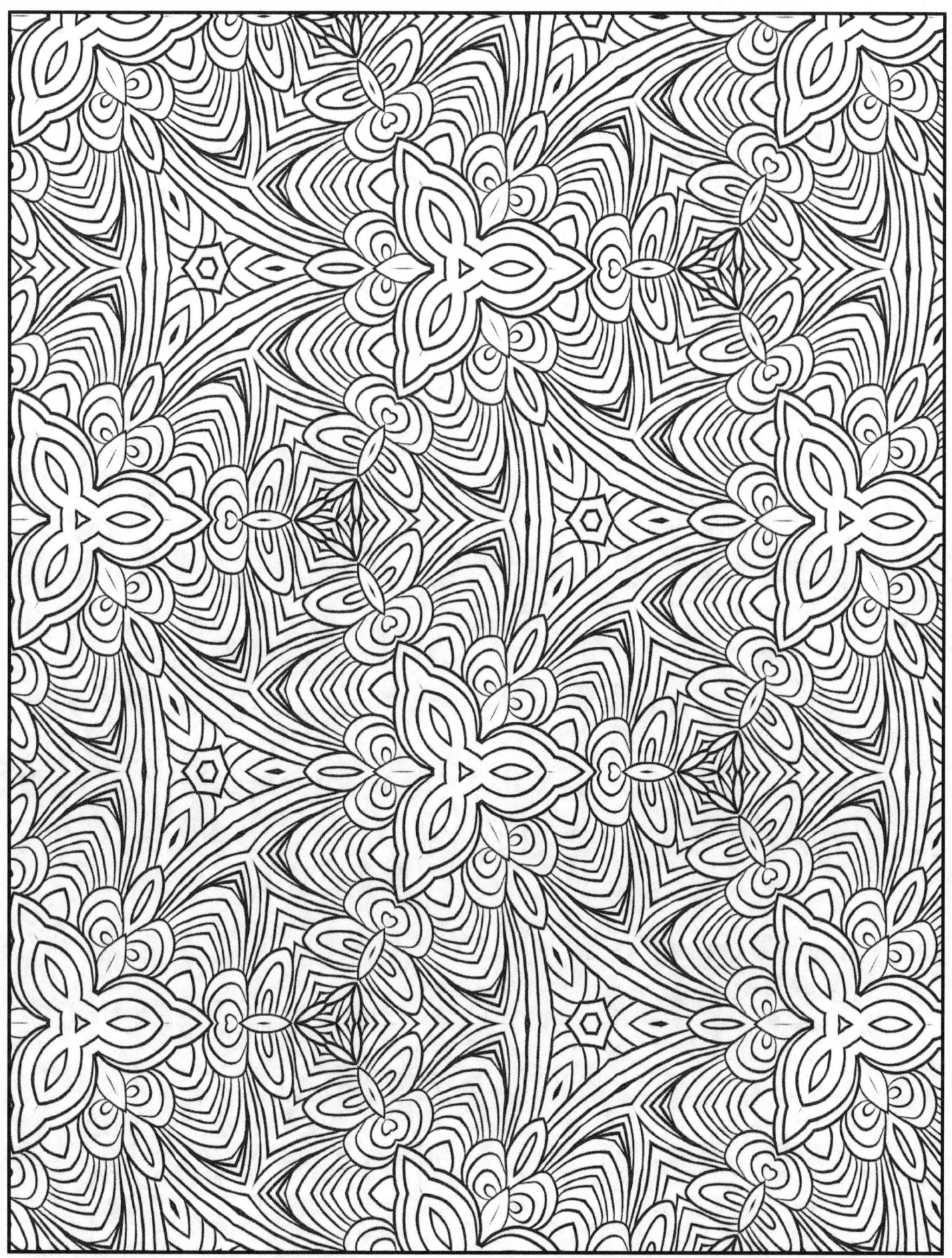

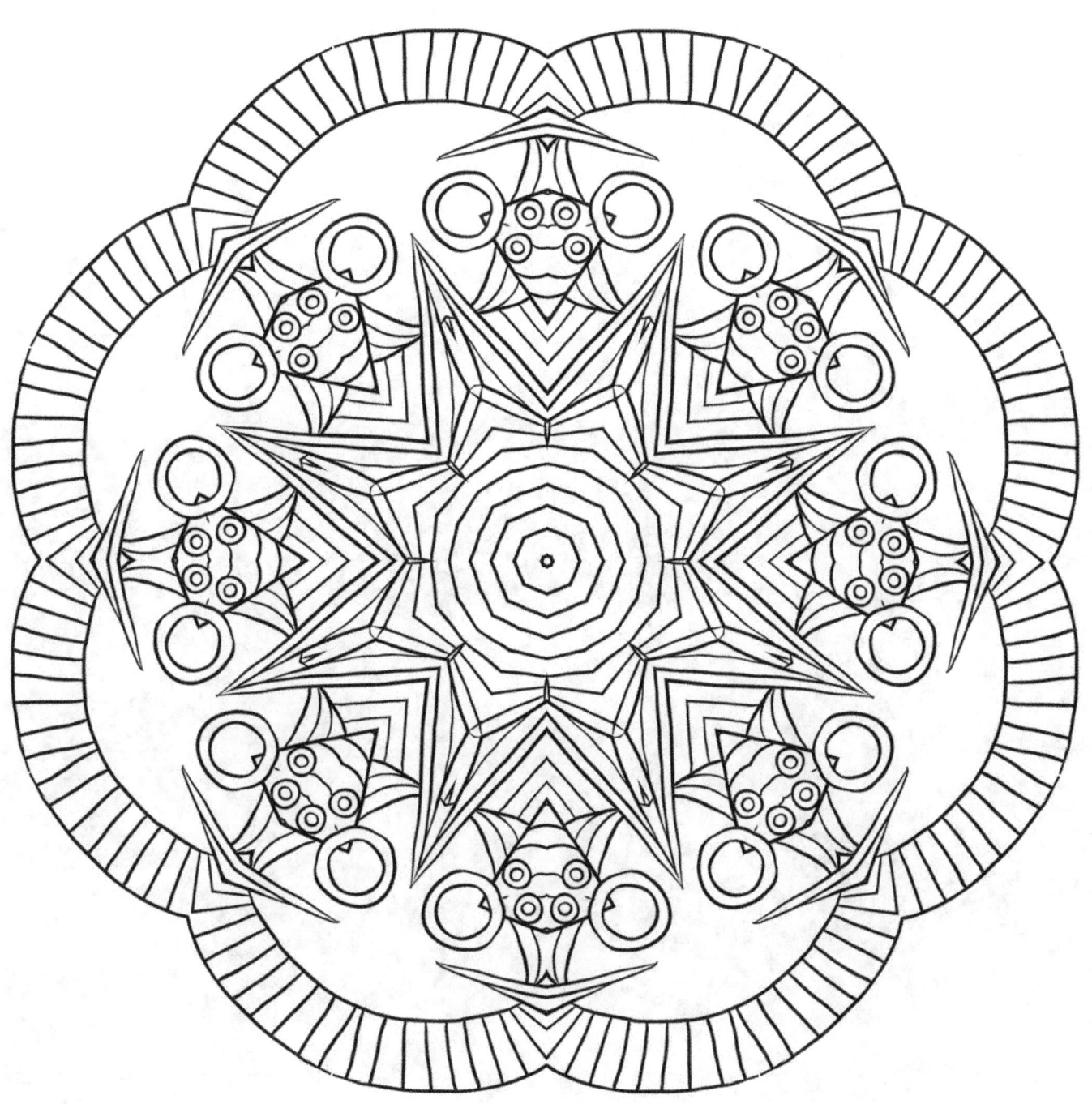

64

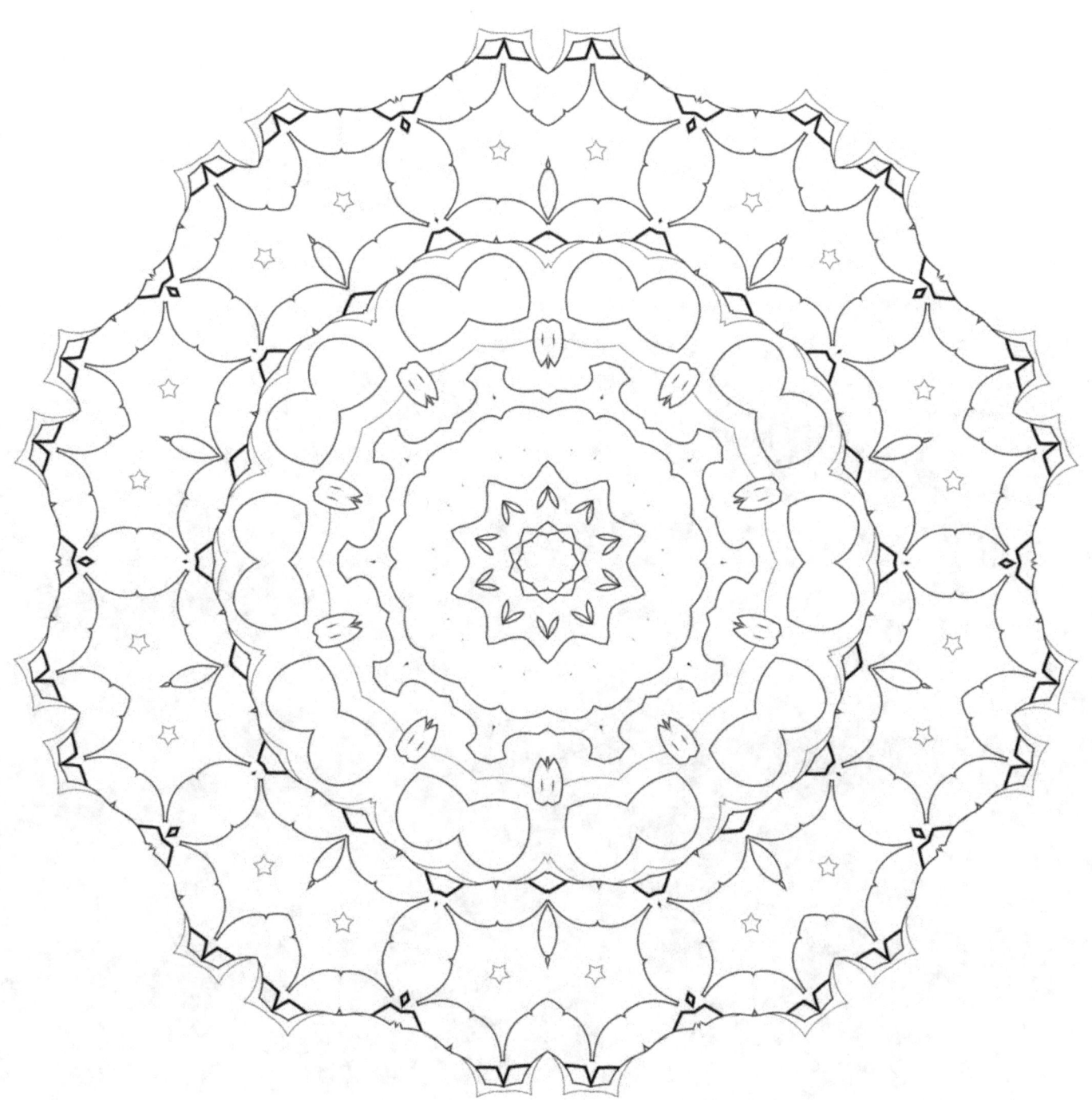

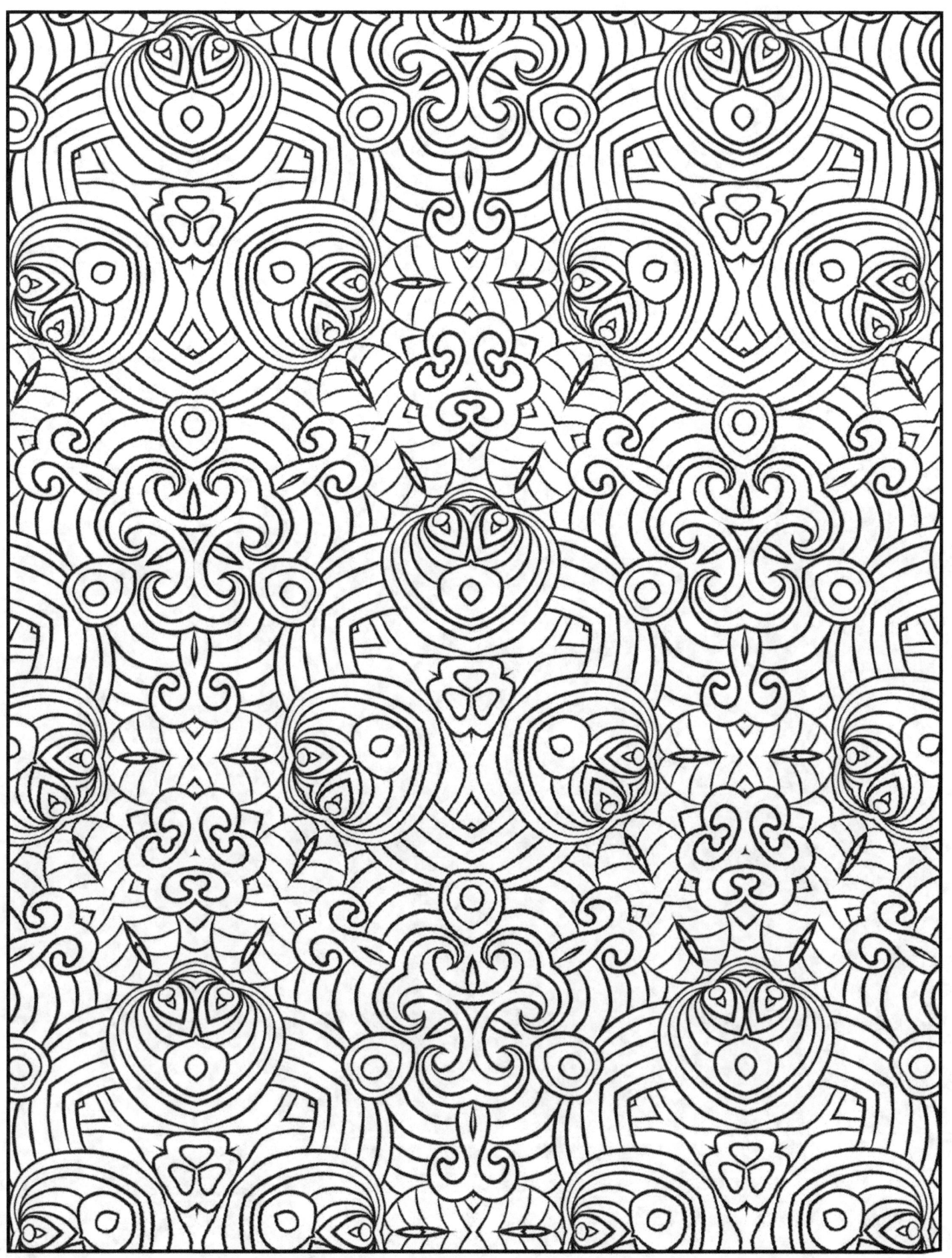

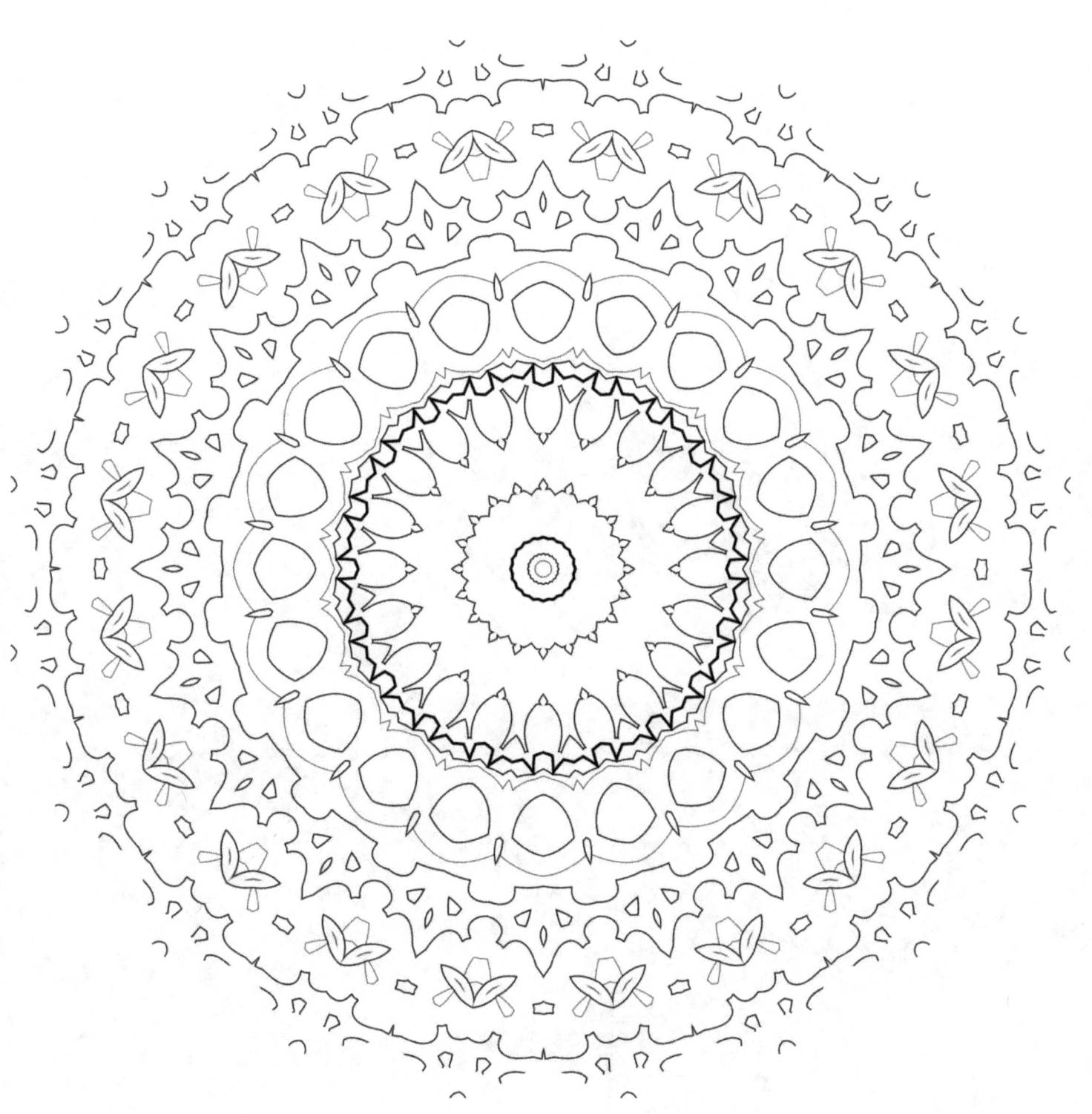

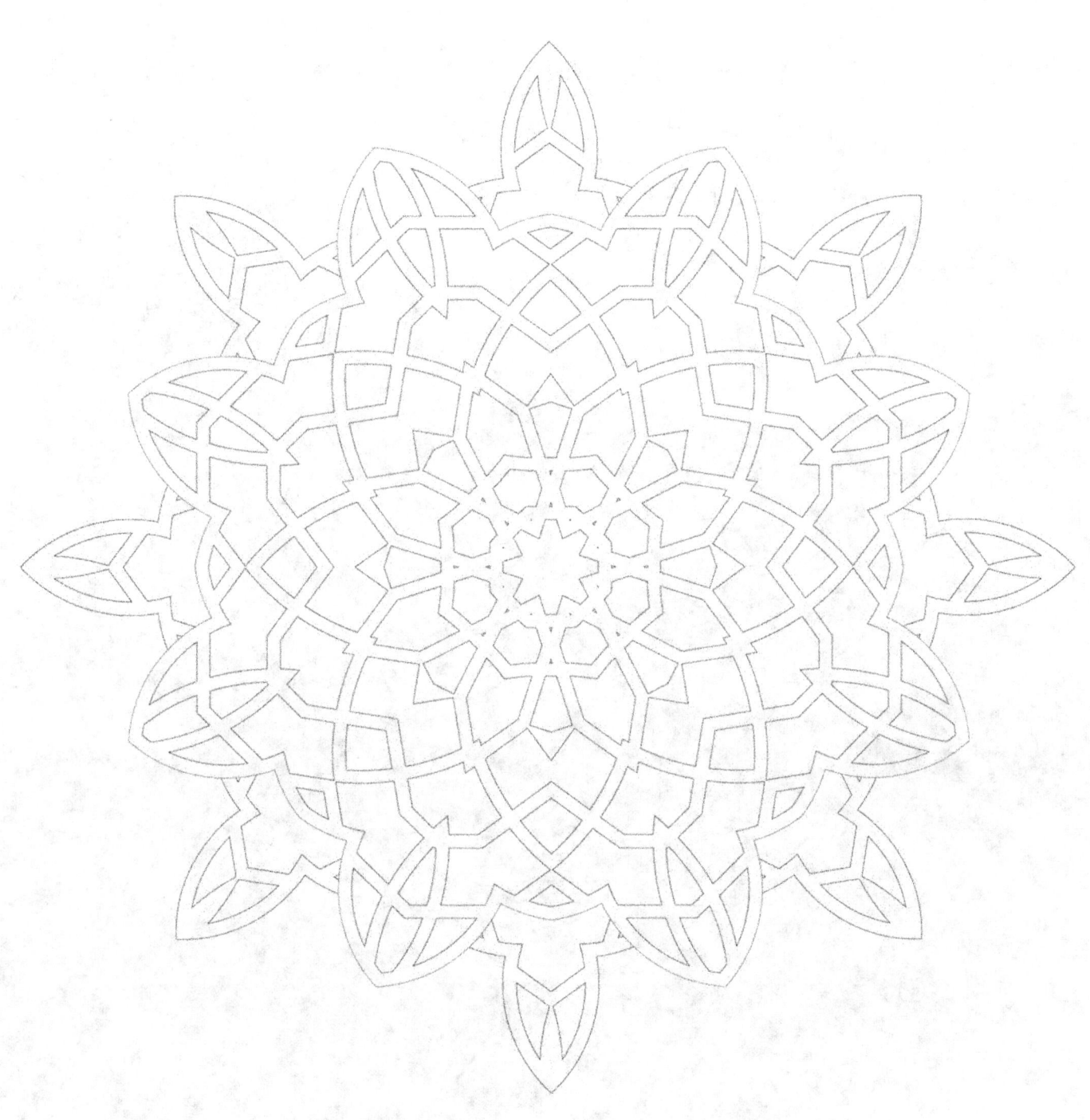

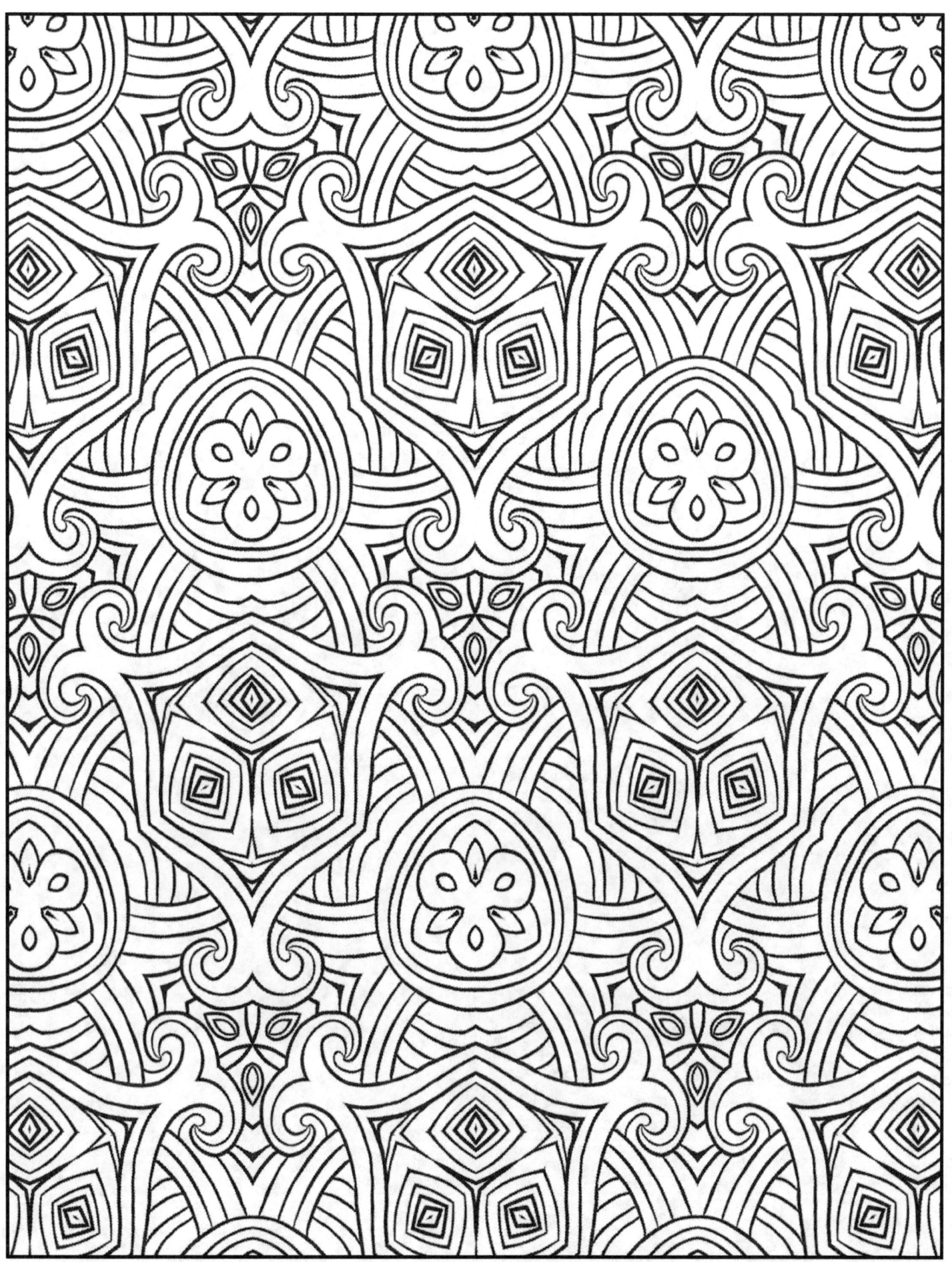

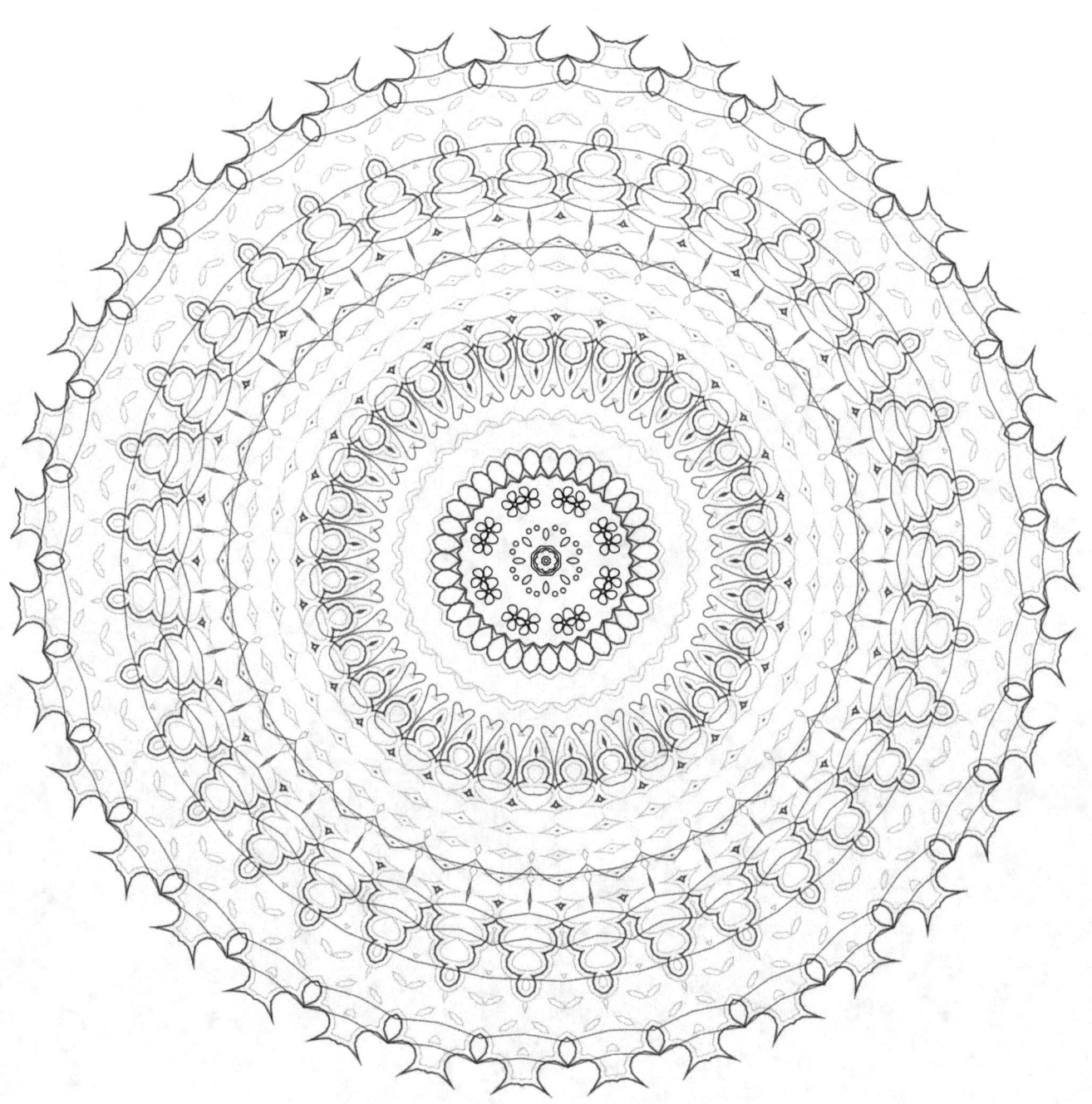

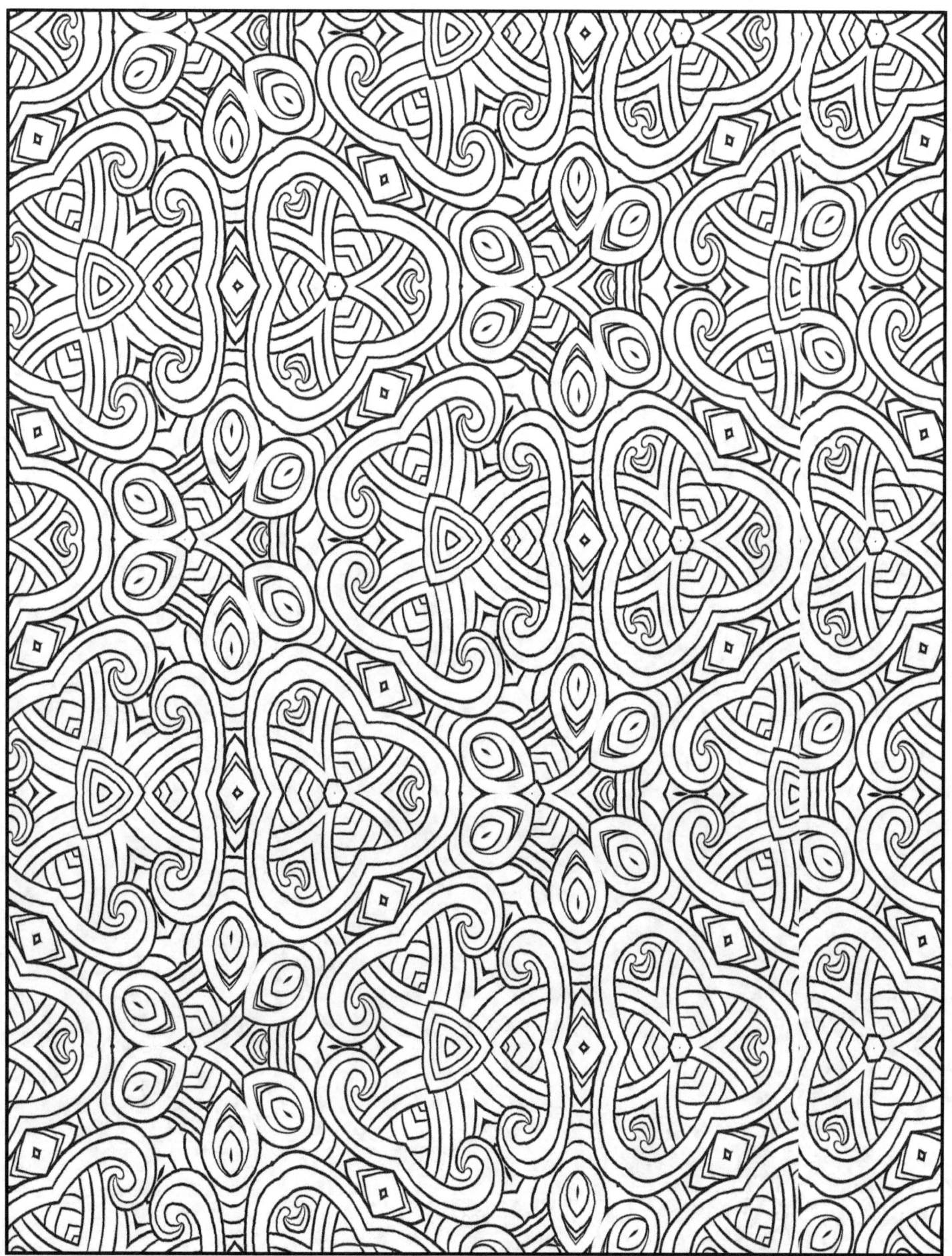

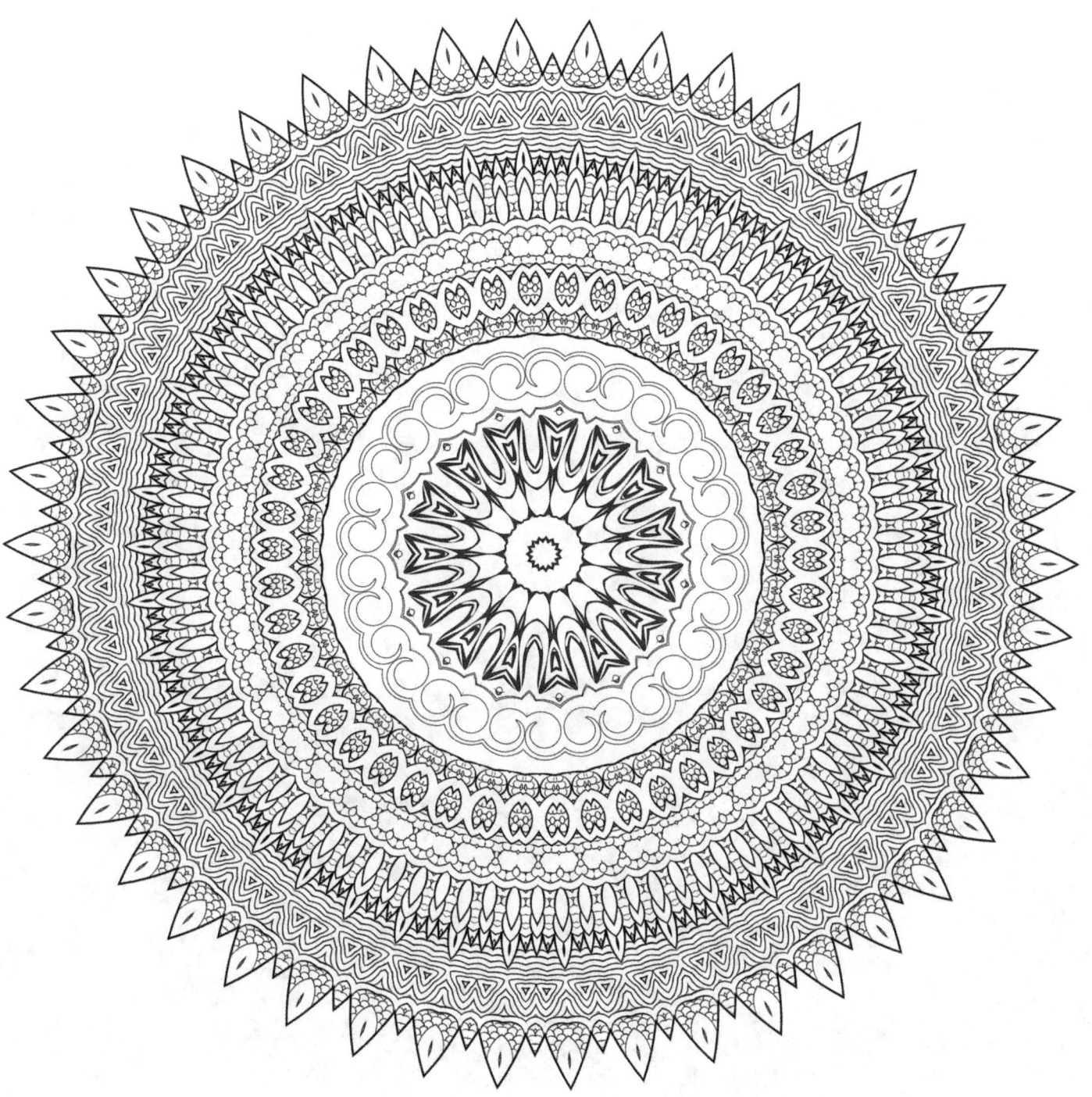

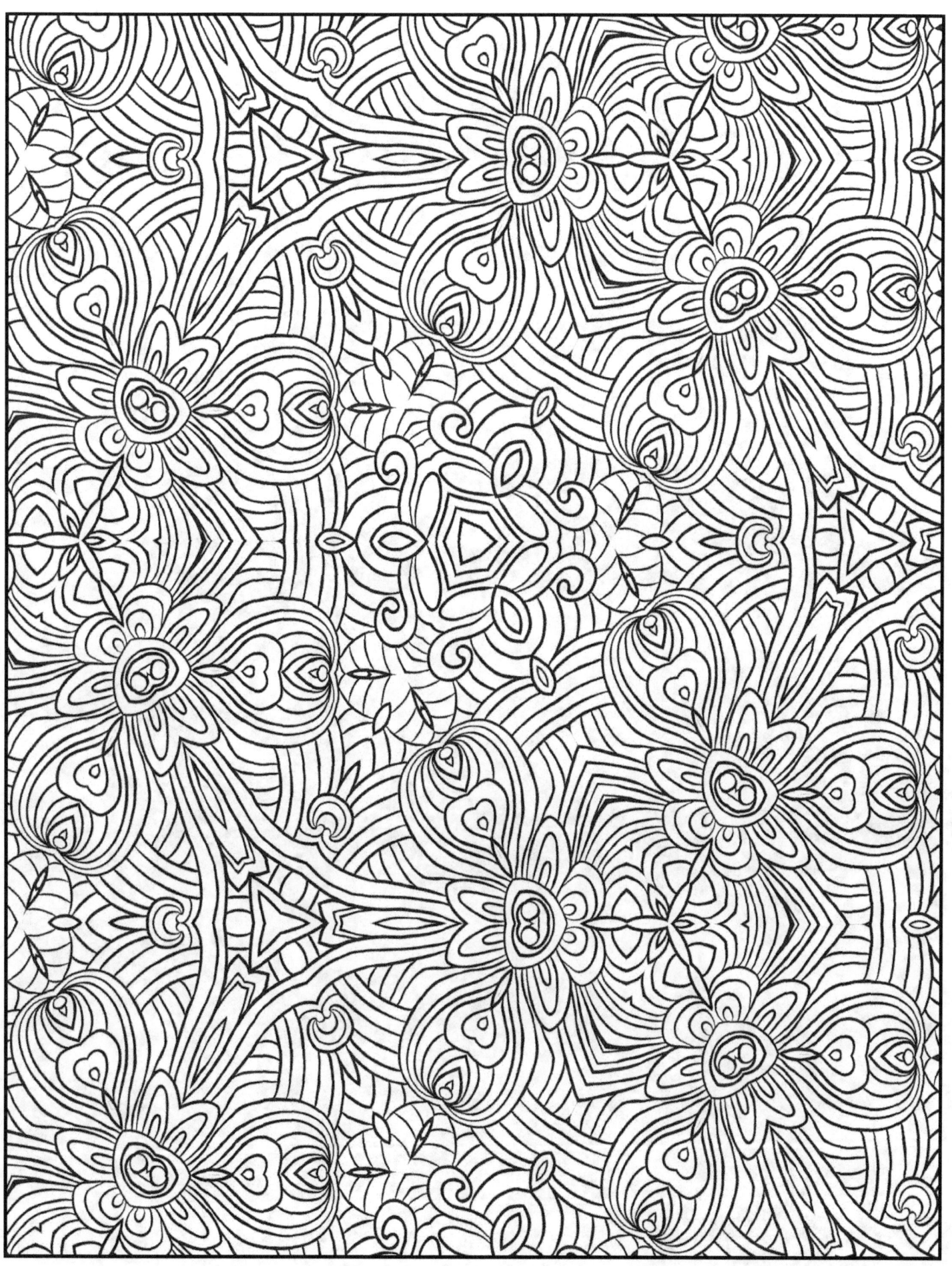

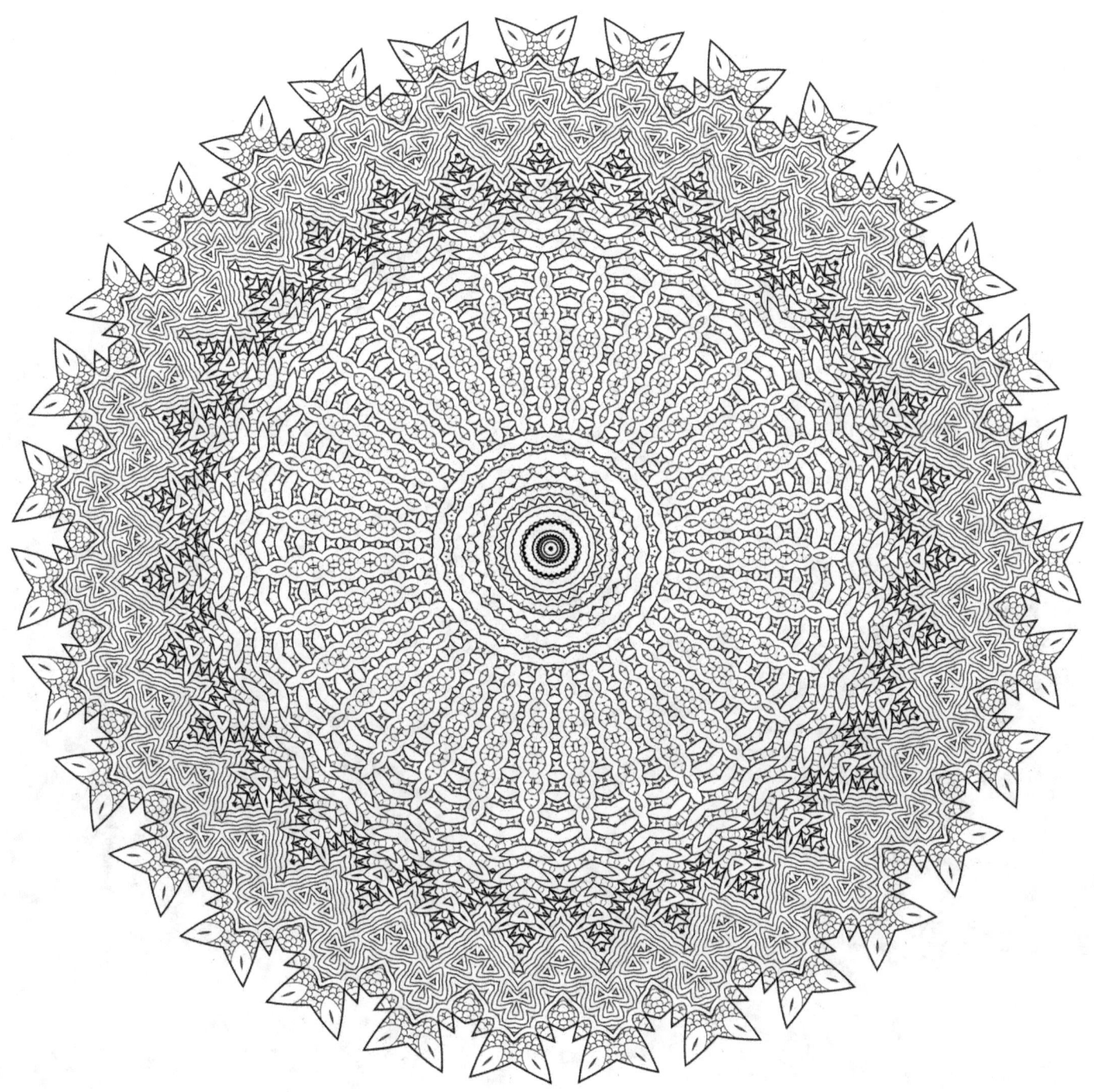

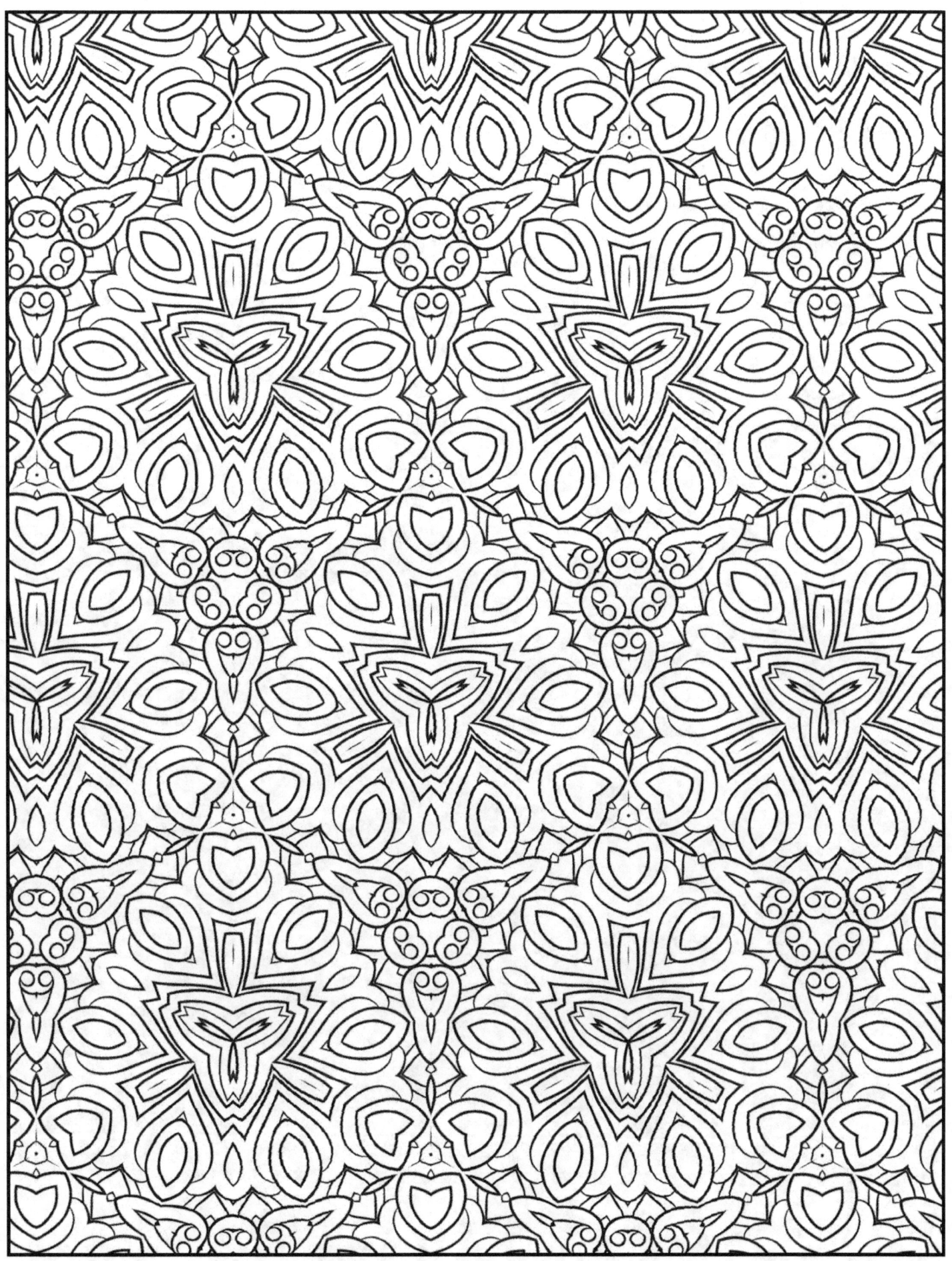

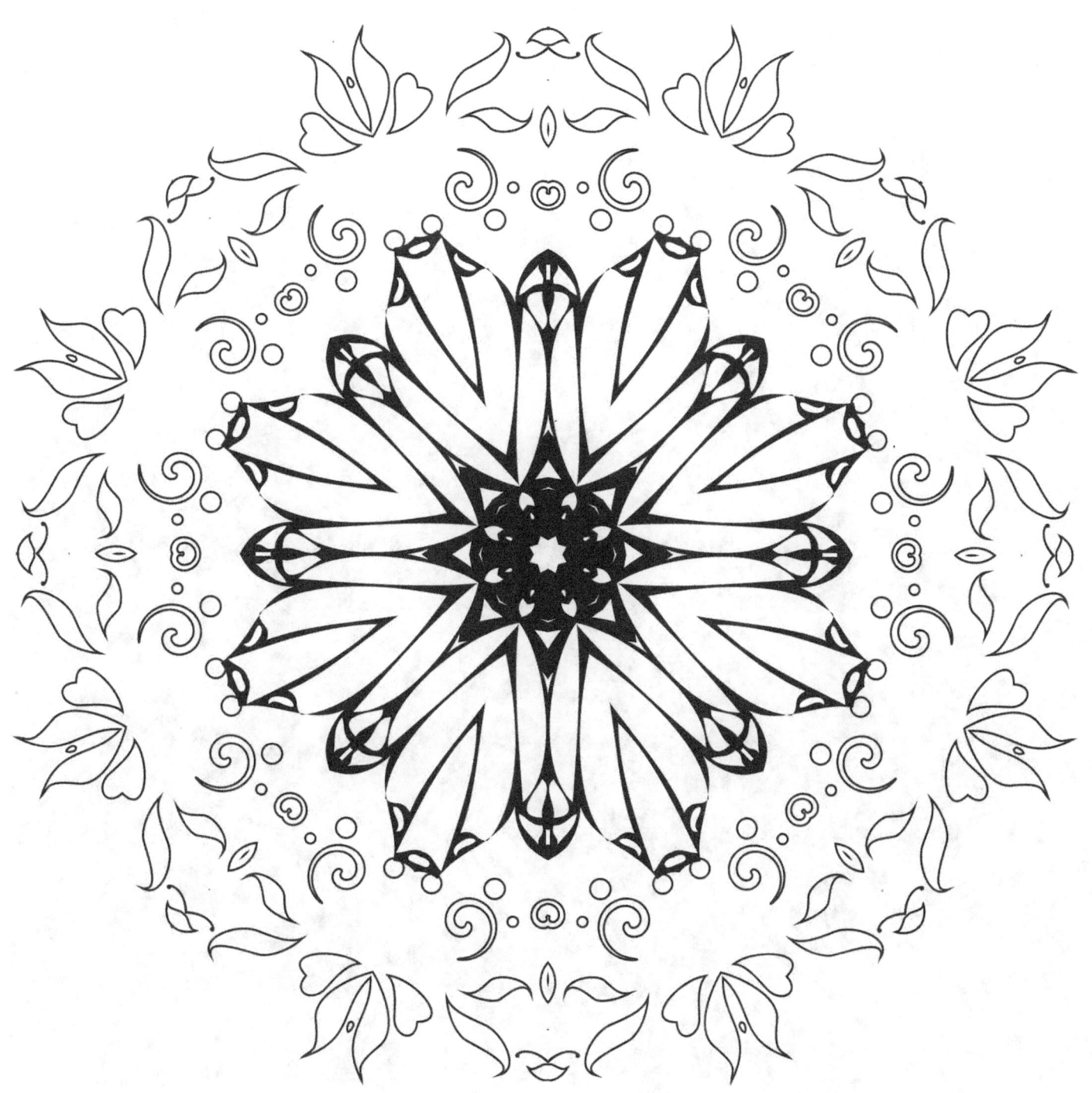

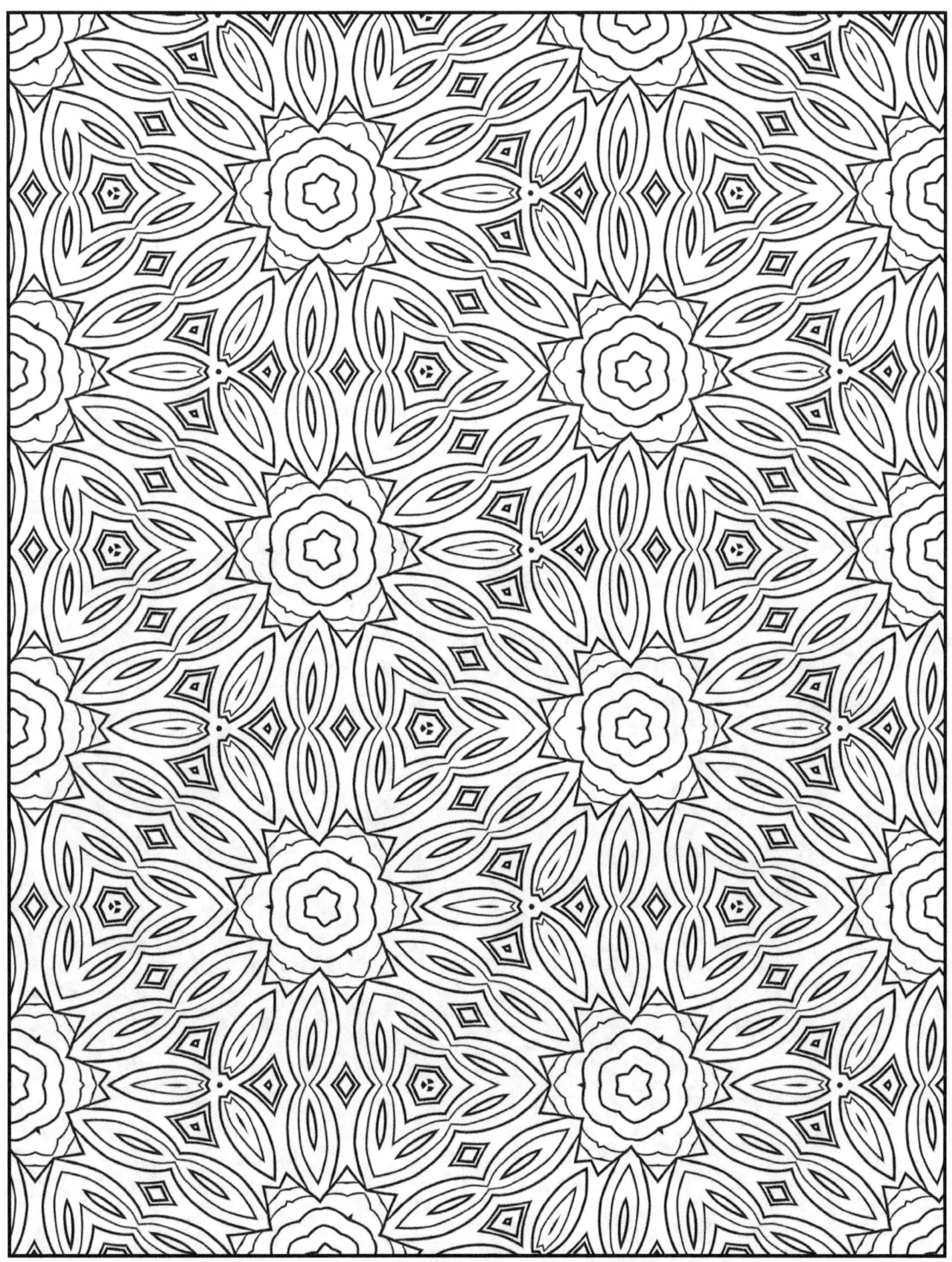

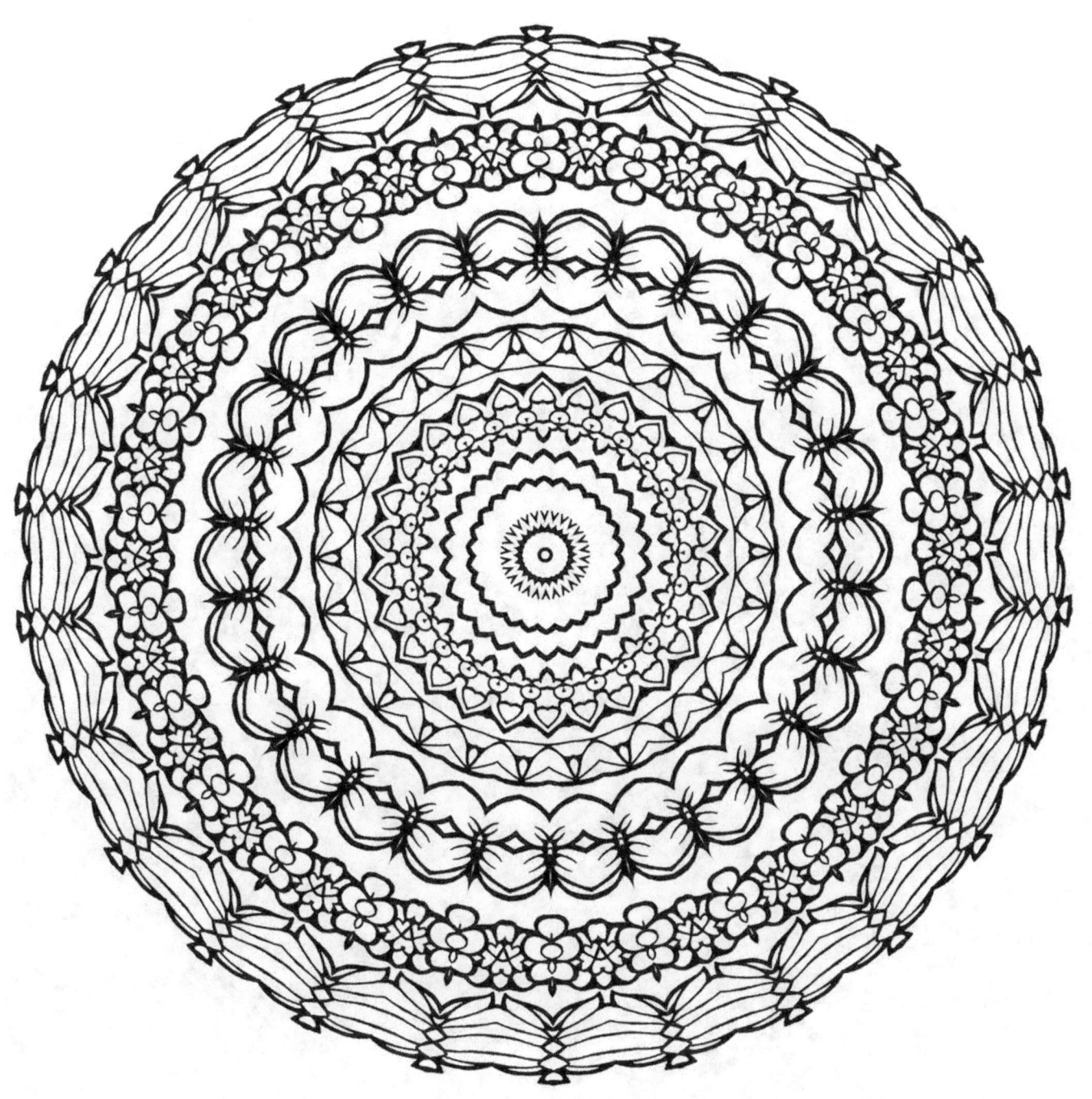

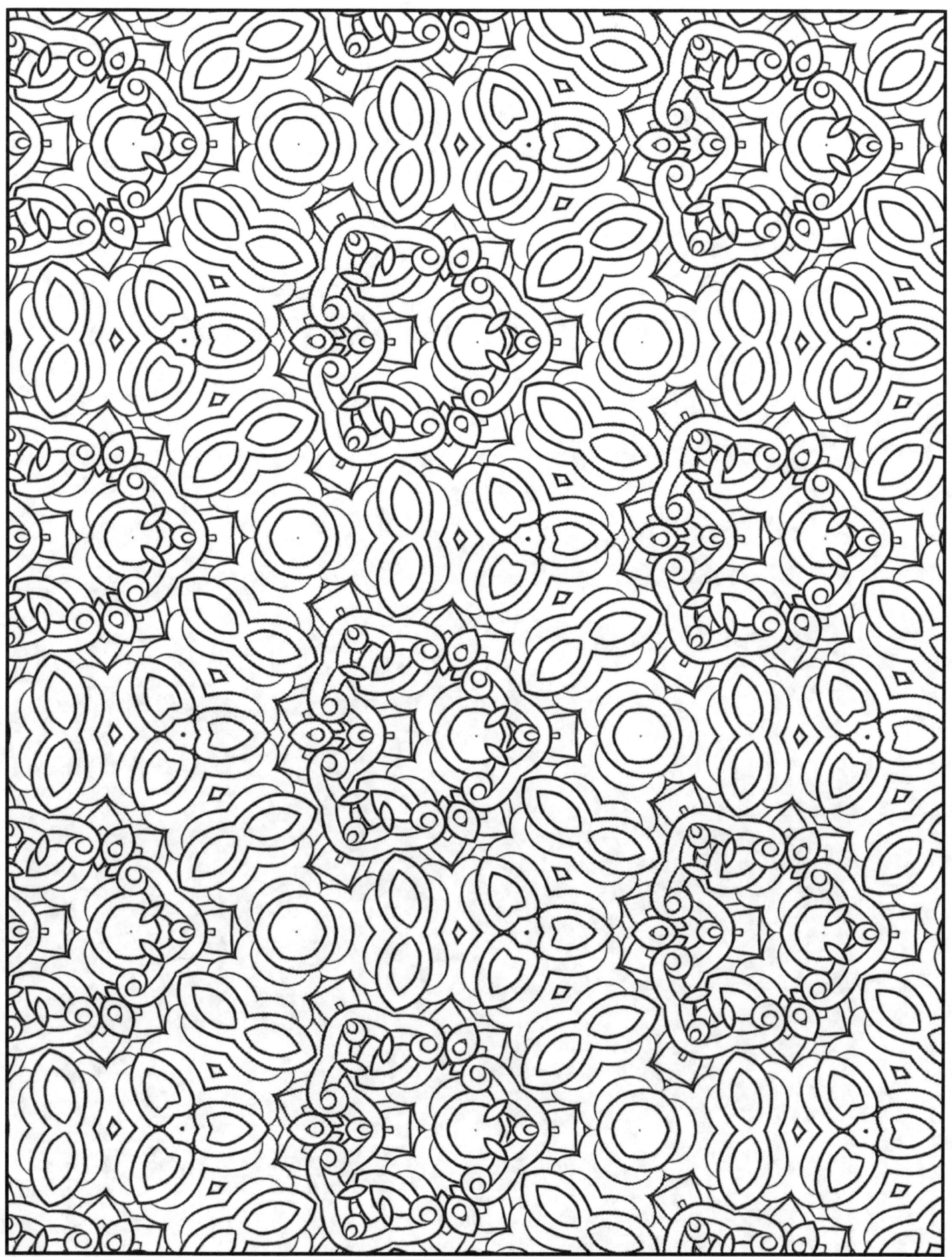

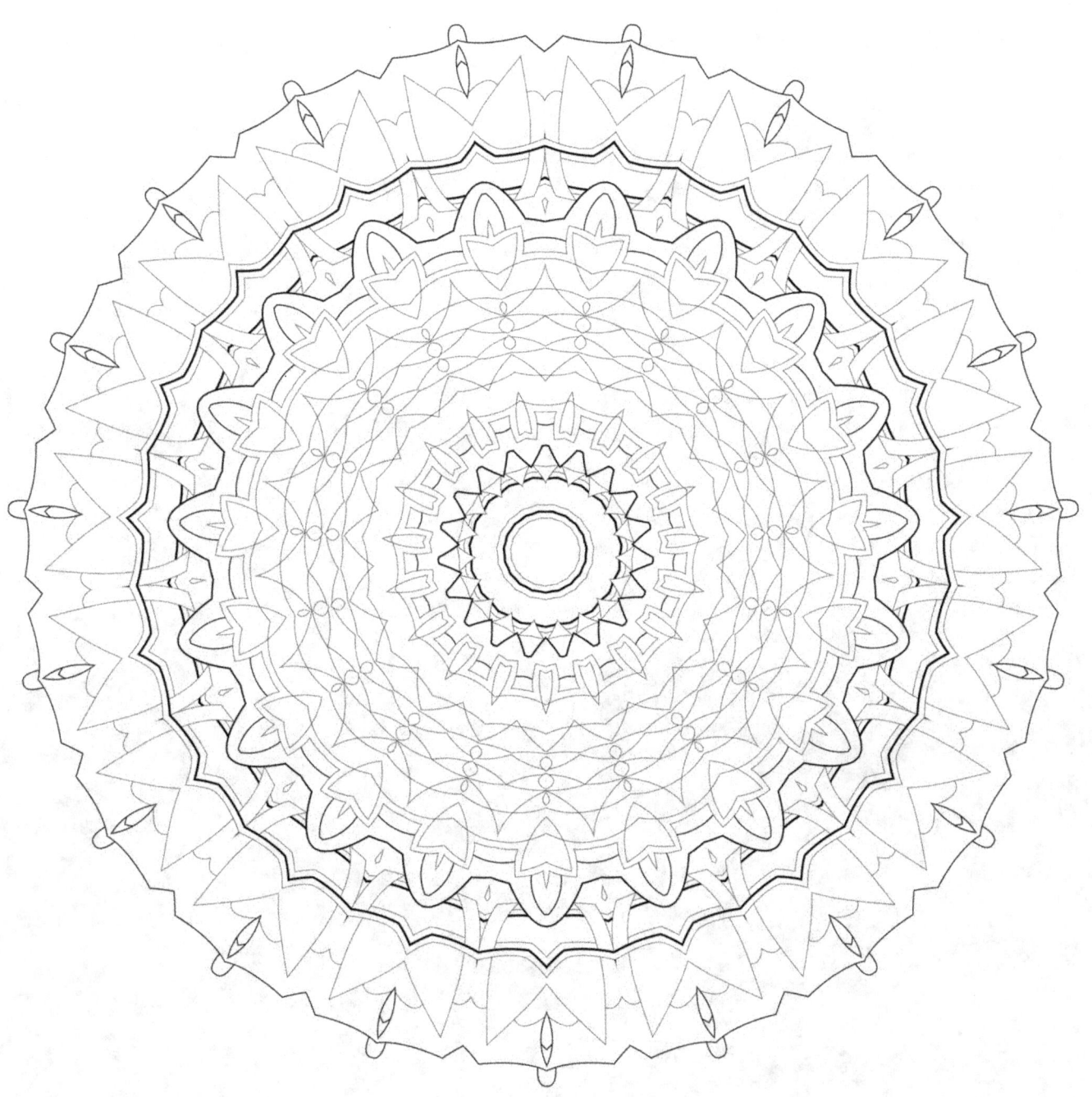

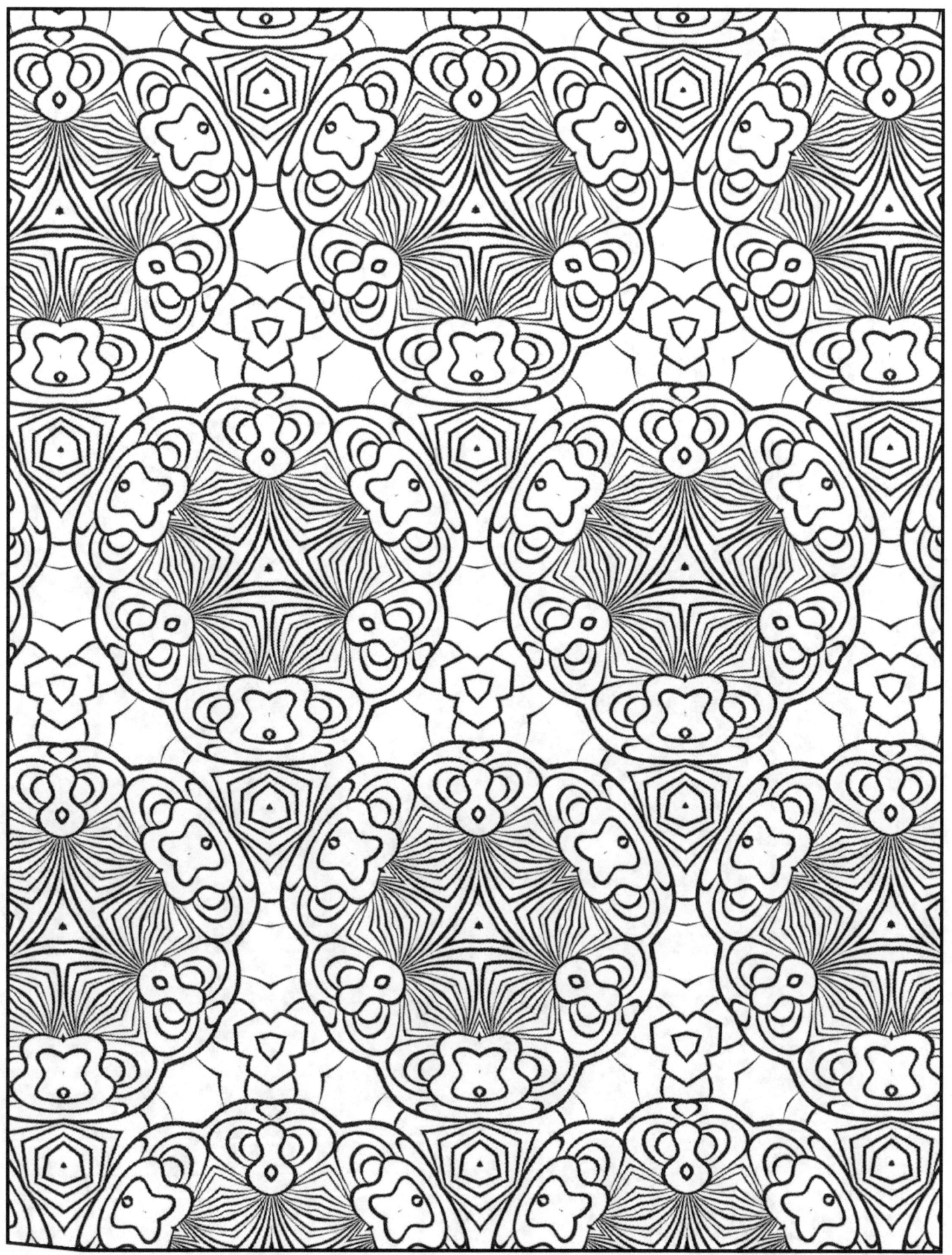

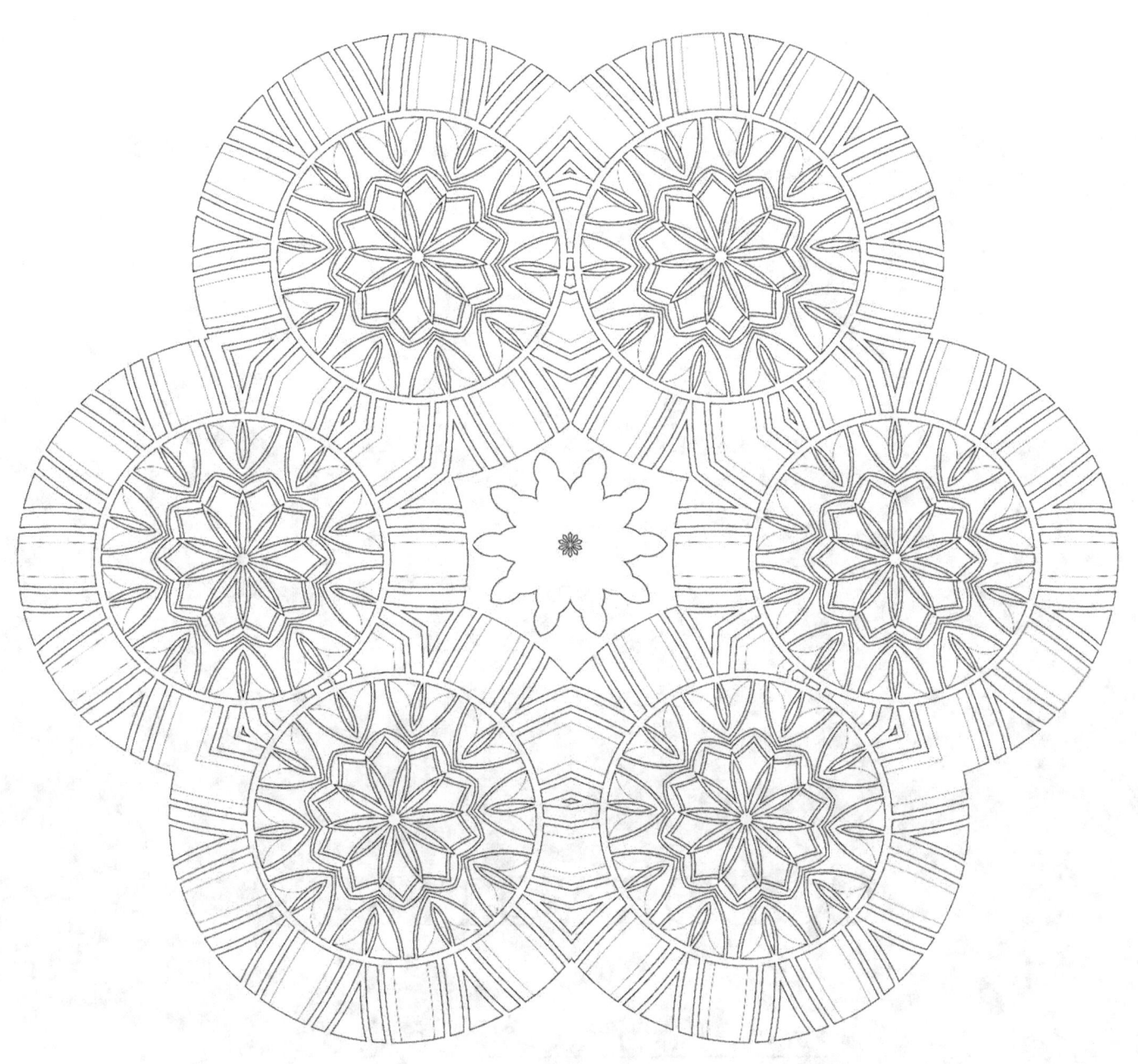

COLOR WITH US

www.LovinkColoring.com

Visit our website for more exclusive coloring pages or books

www.ingramcontent.com/pod-product-compliance
Lightning Source LLC
Chambersburg PA
CBHW080824180526
45168CB00006B/2566